How To Cook In A JIFFY

Even if you have never boiled an egg BEFORE

Prasenjeet Kumar

© Copyright Prasenjeet Kumar 2014

All rights reserved. No part of this book may be reproduced, stored in a retrieval system, or transmitted, in any form or by any means, electronic, mechanical, photocopying, recording or otherwise, without the prior permission of the copyright owner, accept in the case of brief quotations embodied in critical articles or reviews.

We are grateful to you for recognizing and respecting the hard work that this author has put in for bringing out this book.

To economise on costs, this book contains no photographs. However, if you wish to have a look at how the dishes should actually look like, you could either refer to the e-Book version or to the Author's website *www.cookinginajiffy.com*.

For more information, you are welcome to address the author at *ciaj@cookinginajiffy.com*.

What People Say........

"I received a copy of this book from the author in exchange for an honest review. This is a good informative book for someone starting out in the adventure of cooking. This would make a great gift for a young bride just starting out with her new duties of cooking or a single person getting out on their own. In today's busy life parents often don't have the time to teach their kids the important skill of cooking. This book is wrote very easy to understand with clear step by step directions to follow to help you learn the cooking basics. I enjoyed the simplicity of the recipes that were shared and the approach to embrace cooking without worrying about the imperfections that can sometimes happen and just enjoy the end results. It is a wonderful tool to help instill a love of cooking and a healthier approach to a quick and good for you meal in a jiffy!"

B Farrell

ACKNOWLEDGEMENTS

This book (and its partner website *www.cookinginajiffy.com*) is dedicated to my dearest mother who loves not only cooking but also experimenting with food. Despite being a working mother (she is actually a very senior Indian Administrative Service officer), she is an ardent believer in the philosophy that kitchens should be a happy place for families.

She is the sole reason behind the good health and well-being of our entire family. I still remember as a two-year old child, when my mother would be in the kitchen, I would sit on the floor and in a spirit of togetherness, take a toy wok, put in it all the peels of vegetables and stir them feverishly imitating my mother.

Unlike most fathers who would leave their wives to cook food while sitting and watching television, I have seen my father, who too is coincidentally a very senior Indian Administrative Service officer, helping my mother in washing and cutting vegetables, kneading dough and so on, especially in the days when we didn't have reliable domestic help.

This often resulted in meals being cooked from scratch within 30 minutes. And the bonus was that cooking time came to be always celebrated, as family time, with lots of cutting, washing, steaming and frying going on side by side with such planning, co-ordination, and sequencing of operations that would put a Mission to Mars to shame! I, therefore, dedicate this book to my father too, who even now takes time off to "advise" me on what my book should focus on, and sometimes even gives editing suggestions.

To reiterate, dear readers, please note that the recipes compiled in this book (as well as the ones posted on its partner website *www.cookinginajiffy.com*) belong to my mother. She is the original author of all the recipes and NOT ME. I have simply put these out in the public domain to enable others to understand and follow our philosophy of cooking, if they so wish.

I next dedicate this book (and website) to all my friends, relatives and acquaintances who have sampled my mom's cooking either at my home or at my work place from my lunch-box and have pestered me to share those recipes.

Finally, I wish to express my gratitude to all those visitors, fans and followers to my website *www.cookinginajiffy.com* as well as to my Facebook and Twitter pages and for their really encouraging comments and constructive suggestions that have not only kept my morale high in some really frustrating times but have also resulted into the writing of this book.

Table of Contents

I My Story—Why I Had to Learn How to Boil an Egg and Do Much More: 3

II Taking Baby Steps Into The Wonderland Of Cooking: 11

III Who Is This Book Meant For: 21

IV Why Should You Learn Cooking: 25

Lesson 1: How to Set Up Your Very Basic Kitchen: 29

Lesson 2: What Ingredients You Need To Stock and Experiment With: 35

Lesson 3: How to Make Tea Or Coffee: 41

Lesson 4: How to Toast Bread and Graduate to making Bread Crumbs, Garlic Toasts and Cheese Garlic Toasts: 45

Lesson 5: How to Boil and Peel an Egg Flawlessly and Learn to do much more: 49

Lesson 6: How to Cook Your Vegetables: 83

Lesson 7: How to Handle Chicken: 105

Lesson 8: What to Do With Fish and Seafood: 125

Lesson 9: Soups and Salads: 141

Lesson 10: Making a Full Meal in 30 Minutes: with Proper Sequencing and Parallel Processing: 159

Parting Tips....... 175

Other Books by the Author: 181

Connect with the Author: 185

Please review my book: 189

Index: 191

I

MY STORY—WHY I HAD TO LEARN HOW TO BOIL AN EGG AND DO MUCH MORE

I was 20 years old and was literally on cloud nine. I had an offer for admission into the prestigious BA (LLB) Honours course of the University College London (UCL), one of the top most Universities in the world. For studying my dream course of Law, with a degree that is "recognized" in India, there just couldn't be a greater place.

Like any other happy go lucky man, I didn't know cooking. This is not considered a "life threatening disease" because at home, in India, cooking is mostly done by domestic help. They were generally trained by my mother into churning out the kind of dishes that we liked.

My mother had learnt some cooking from her mother. But she loved reading cookbooks, downloading recipes from various websites, and experimenting with various cuisines. Many times she would even experiment with nouvelle cuisine that she would come across in a fancy restaurant abroad.

UCL had a wide variety of accommodation. Most of them were self-catered and only two were catered halls. Since I didn't know any cooking, I exercised extraordinary care to opt for only catered halls in the application form and crossed out all the non-catered or self-catered options.

After a couple of months, I was informed, to my great relief, that my application for a catered hall was SUCCESSFUL. I was allocated Ifor Evans, a Hall Of Residence, located in Camden Town.

Came 20 September 2005 and I landed at London Heathrow after a grueling nine-hour non-stop flight from India. Immediately I had to get into an extremely long queue for immigration. It was 6:00 in the evening (which was 11.30 pm by Indian Standard time).

My turn at the immigration counter came after about an hour. I handed over my passport and caught a furtive glance at the form that the Immigration Officer was scribbling on. My heart did skip a beat or two because the form had such ominous choices as "Arrest Him"; "Deport Him" and so on. The officer, however, had just a cursory look at my documents and instead of asking any tricky questions, congratulated me for doing such a great job by gaining admission at UCL.

Then he remarked that since this meant that I would be spending more than six months in the UK, I needed to see a doctor. I was puzzled. After all, it did sound like that if you planned to be spending more than six months in the UK, and that too during the winters, you certainly needed to get your head examined by a doctor at the Heathrow airport!!!

Anyway, I had no option but to join another long queue, this time outside the Heathrow Medical Services office. I saw students, mostly from countries in the Far East, India, Africa and South American countries, waiting patiently for their turn. I soon learnt that it was not my head but my chest that interested them. This was going to be x-rayed to diagnose whether any of us students from the developing part of the world was suffering from tuberculosis!

It was then that I suddenly remembered the advice of one of my friends, who had studied in London before, to bring along a recent chest x-ray.

This seemed strange to me but nevertheless, I had got my chest x-rayed in India. As I was unaware of what was going to happen to me at London

Heathrow airport, I had packed that x-ray carefully in my checked-in baggage. That was certainly a BIG mistake.

I soon learnt with trepidation that if you didn't have an x-ray of your chest when you arrived in the United Kingdom, you had to be x-rayed right there and then at the Airport. And this process could take up to 5-7 hours as the queue would be very long. I really cursed myself for not having kept the chest x-ray readily accessible in my hand baggage.

Anyway, when my turn came and that too after an hour and a half, I was asked by the Medical Services officer whether I ever had a chest x-ray done. I told her that I was carrying a chest x-ray from my home country but that was unfortunately in my checked-in baggage.

Instead of scowling or scolding, the Doctor to my relief was actually very helpful. She immediately gave me a card, so that I could access my checked-in baggage at the Baggage Reclaim. I quickly ran to that area and located my baggage.

It appeared to be in a reasonably good condition, except for the very strong tape all-around it that the Indian airport security had put in routine to probably dissuade anyone planning to slip in a bomb or two in my luggage. The problem was that you needed something sharp like a knife to cut through that tape, and you can't carry any such sharp instrument in your hand baggage. Quite a Catch-22 situation, I must say.

The only "sharp" thing I appeared to have in my possession were my luggage keys. So I had no option but to use those suitcase keys to patiently saw through the tape to reach my x-ray.

I then rushed back to the Medical officer who after seeing my x-ray finally let me go. I later learnt that the British Government was, on an average, spending GBP 100 on each such x-ray at Heathrow, and was mighty pleased to save that much expenditure of the Government right after my arrival.

A friend had already come to pick me up from the airport. He too had been patiently waiting for nearly three hours. I was constantly in touch with him (thanks to the wonders of mobile telephony), as well as with my parents in India who just couldn't sleep with tension. Ifor Evans was another 45 minutes' drive from the London Heathrow airport.

When I checked in at Ifor Evans, the security guard (there was no reception at 10 o' clock in the night in any case, plus it was also a Sunday) just handed me the keys to my room with a catalogue of information (such as life at UCL or living in London). I was so exhausted that I could barely make it to my bed and crashed.

The next morning, still groggy and jet lagged, I couldn't first recall why I was in such a strange and unfamiliar place. After taking a shower and changing into fresh clothes, I decided to look for the Dining Room but didn't know where it was.

I had only seen the building during night time and knew that I was on the third floor. Now I had to figure a way out, quite like the way prisoners try to escape from medieval dungeons in Hollywood movies.

I finally managed to get out of the building and followed my nose to the wafting smell of frying eggs to the Dining Room. And then my world, along with all my "due diligence" in finding me a catered Hall of Residence came crashing down.

Yes, I had come to the right Dining Room, in the Ifor Evans Hall. Yes, breakfast was still being served. But, no, I couldn't have it.

Why??? God, I had already passed my immigration and x-ray tests and was willing to get my head examined too. But no, the kind souls in the Dining Room were not willing to relent.

The dining room was open at Ifor Evans only for tourists, and NOT for lowly creatures like students.

Why? Because the UCL Autumn Term had officially not begun. Ok, charge me extra, I pleaded. No, I was told very clearly that students were not allowed to eat at the dining room even if they were willing to pay extra.

Why? Because the caterers had not planned for that exigency.

But as international students, I tried to resubmit my case, we were specifically asked to arrive a week in advance before the commencement of the First Term which was at the end of September. This was meant to settle international students well before the start of their respective courses.

That may be fine, I was answered. However, no meals were to be served during that one week period because the Hall of Residence staff was technically on leave as the term had not begun.

As a budding lawyer, I had just lost my first case.

And with this my rites of passage in the Find Me a Meal ritual in the Wonderland of Cooking had just begun.

II

TAKING BABY STEPS INTO THE WONDERLAND OF COOKING

Angry and confused, and suffering from terrible hunger pangs because the last meal that the airlines had served me was some 18 hours back, I had no option but to hit the streets.

The friendly lady at the Reception told me that Camden Town was bustling with delis and eating out options. After wandering about for some 500 meters, I found a small supermarket express, with its signboard, shining from a distance, the same way as a ship looking for land may spot a lighthouse.

The express shop had a wide variety of sandwiches on offer. After going through the various options, I decided to go for a Tuna sandwich. I also ordered a cup of coffee. That will be 4 Pounds, the cashier said. I gulped with astonishment. 4 Pounds meant 320 Indian Rupees---which could get me a sandwich and coffee in the canteen of my old college in Delhi for at least 20 days!

There was nothing great about the sandwiches. They were soulless and tasted "plasticky", if you know what I mean. But at least they were convenient.

For lunch, I decided to visit a nearby deli. It served decent Panini but that was much more expensive than the sandwiches. The difference was that at least I got something warm to eat.

This went on for a full week till I was allowed entry into the Dining Room of Ifor Evans. I thus had to survive on all kinds of sandwiches, tortillas, wraps and salads (various kinds of pasta and egg salads with mayonnaise, lettuce, mustard, etc) for this entire miserable period. I was getting poorer and poorer and was missing my home food terribly.

Coming back to my room, I would open up all my Guide Books and plough through the instructions. When I went through the fine print, I realized to my horror that all UCL catered halls had ONE RULE (perhaps like most other colleges in the University of London and various other Universities in the United Kingdom, but unlike any "catered" college in India). And can you guess what that rule could be??????????

The rule was that all meals were provided EXCEPT LUNCHES ON ALL DAYS AND ALL MEALS ON WEEKENDS. That meant going back to the dreaded sandwiches and salads for the lunches and the weekends. I couldn't bear the thought.

One of the Guide Books somewhat helpfully suggested that international students should learn cooking before arriving in Britain. Back in India, I had once tried to learn cooking some Indian dishes like rice and dal (lentils) in my spare time but noticed that both these preparations required a pressure cooker. I couldn't carry a pressure cooker to the UK for the simple reason that there is a limitation on how much weight you can carry in your luggage in an airline.

Another reason was that I had to carry my bedding (minus the mattress thankfully!) along with my clothes, especially winter clothes. This was because Ifor Evans had given us two options: either carry your own bedding or pay fifty pounds to the Hall of Residence for it.

Most international students being on a tighter budget like me naturally preferred to carry their own bedding. So, there was not really much space left for carrying kitchen equipment except for a few crockery and cutlery.

Ifor Evans fortunately had a very decent kitchen on every floor. The kitchen was equipped with a few ovens, fridges and cooking stoves. For my first miserable week, I had not really used the kitchen much except for storing my sandwiches in the fridge. Now after realizing that I'd have to be on my own during all weekends and holidays, I had to be open to newer ideas.

Then one day I met a student from Portugal who too looked lost just like me. I showed him around and pointed out the places where from he could buy some food. He told me that he was not very fond of sandwiches or salads and wanted to have something warm.

So, then we ventured out, this time in the opposite direction and soon found a proper supermarket. We bought baking trays for 99 pence each. My friend did not know cooking, quite like me. He told me that at home, his mom used to do the cooking. We bought some lasagna.

I had never heated food before and was a little hesitant to use the ovens in the Ifor Evans kitchen. The packaged product had, however, very easy-to-follow cooking instructions including how to puncture the plastic film, how to place the product inside the baker and at what temperature to cook that dish for how many minutes. We followed the instructions diligently and were relieved when the package neither exploded nor burnt our fingers. This was the first time I learnt how to heat up a readymade meal in an oven.

Apart from this single baking tray, I did not have any other cooking utensil. The first few weekends I lived simply like this. I was grateful for the warm breakfast and dinner that I could have at Ifor Evans during the week days.

For lunches, I still had to be on my own. I lived on sandwiches, cereals, sometimes heated readymade roast chicken. I usually did not have any greens. Sometimes I would even forget to have lunch because I would be busy attending tutorials and lectures, making notes in the library or participating in such extracurricular activities as mooting.

After three months, when I flew back to India for my winter vacations, my friends and family members were quite shocked to see me. I looked pale and skinny and was quite a couple of kilos lighter. My mom asked me what I had done to myself. My father joked about the "greatness" of the UCL Slimming Centre and "recommended" its services to all and sundry. It was obvious that I was not having proper nutritious food.

When I was going back to London for my Second Term, my mom insisted that I carry along a pan. (This was despite telling my mom that I did not need a pan and was happy with whatever I was doing). This was the second kitchen utensil I acquired (the baking tray being the first).

One Sunday I thought of experimenting with boiling an egg that, don't laugh, I had never done before. I called up my mom (thanks to Skype/Google Talk) and diligently wrote down the instructions for boiling an egg, including what to put in the pan first water or egg; how much water to put; how to get a half-boiled egg and so on. My mom also gave me some tips on how to peel a boiled egg flawlessly that I didn't know.

I bought some eggs from the supermarket that day. I was excited to experiment as well as a little afraid of the consequences. Surprisingly, the experiment went off rather well. I was able to have a perfectly boiled and peeled egg for breakfast without any problems. (I am sharing more details regarding this story in Lesson 5--How to boil an egg and graduate to various egg recipes.)

This literally opened the doors for further experimentation. A good thing about Ifor Evans was that since a lot of students were cooking in the kitchen, it was helpful in soothing frayed nerves and in taking out the performance anxiety.

Whenever I wanted to cook anything, I would ring up mom and write down instructions. I learnt to sauté veggies, starting with sautéing peas for breakfast (the way I used to have them in India for breakfast) and then graduating to sautéing other vegetables like carrots, cauliflower, mushroom, spinach, etc. I thus started having veggies in all my meals and was hopeful that with my vitamins replenished, no one will now ever call me "pale".

Learning to boil a perfect egg now led to many more possibilities. I learnt to make an egg sandwich by mashing the same boiled eggs. Once I learnt to make a sandwich, I could make any kind of sandwich whether it was with egg, ham, or with plain lettuce, cucumber and tomatoes.

When I became even more confident, I started experimenting with chicken. I learnt to boil chicken just the way I had learnt to boil an egg. Then I graduated to baking chicken, making chicken in white sauce, etc. When I became even more adventurous, I experimented with some sea food. I cooked prawns in a nice tomato sauce and had it with corn and other veggies.

I was overjoyed with the fact that I could cook proper meals from scratch without anyone, including a domestic help, hovering over me and offering me a helping hand.

This was my first stint with cooking and I found cooking to be absolutely magic. Raw chicken, fish, prawns and vegetables--all look so different. But when I tossed them in a pan with butter, the colours would magically change. Raw prawns are grey in colour but when cooked they get a bright red colour. Raw peas have a dull green colour but when you start sautéing, they acquire a bright green colour which is soothing to the eye. The same thing I noticed about carrots, mushrooms, etc. And then the aroma of things sautéing in pure butter, was simply divine!

Spinach was my favourite veggie when I was in India. I enjoyed spinach, when cooked the Indian way, even when I was a small child. I suppose, a little bit of credit for this should go to the cartoon character Popeye who used to develop big bulging biceps by just feeding on canned spinach. But when I started cooking spinach, I found it to be quite a magical and majestic vegetable. I now noticed how raw spinach looks like leaves of a tree. However, when you cook it, it leaves a lot of water losing its leaf like look and instead gaining a small thread kind of an appearance. I was surprised to find that a 500 gram packet of spinach, when cooked, could be reduced to a serving size for barely one person. I experimented later on with putting goat cheese, and fresh crème to make it even tastier.

Ultimately, like my mother, I fell in love with cooking. Cooking was no longer drudgery. It was a really nice way to take a break from my studies.

Though I never considered myself to be even close to a professional chef, others slowly started noticing my culinary skills. A guy was so impressed seeing me having nice colourful sautéed vegetables for lunch along with my main meal, that he couldn't help asking me whether I had cooked the vegetables myself. When I answered in the affirmative, he told me that I was having a very civilized lunch and that I should not tell my future wife that I was such a good cook. I accepted his compliment with whatever humility I could muster but I thought it to be a little too much especially the part of keeping my "culinary skills" a secret from my future wife!

In the end, I was happy and grateful that I could make nutritious meals even at my Hall of Residence with such limited resources. I was no longer dependent on having sub-standard sandwiches and salads from supermarkets and delis.

I don't think I will ever become a great chef who can cook anything and everything. But I was confident that I could now be a master of my nutritional needs wherever my studies or work or even vacations took me. I think the secret is to focus on all the things that you like eating and then to keep your cooking simple, subtle and eminently manageable.

The lesson: If such a novice like me could manage cooking, so can anyone.

III

WHO IS THIS BOOK MEANT FOR

First of all, this book is meant for all my college friends who are about to start their University education and are going to live by themselves, probably for the first time in their lives, in self-catered dorms, hostels, halls of residence, apartments, whatever.

They either starve themselves or survive on street food--- sandwiches from supermarkets, instant noodles that you can have straightaway (that you don't even need to boil) etc etc.... In the process, they become deficient in vitamins, minerals, proteins and a lot of other good stuff, which is not really a good state to be in when you need to muster all your resources for excelling in your chosen courses of study.

Next, it is addressed to all those newly employed people who are about to start their careers in

Mumbai, Dubai, Singapore, London, New York or elsewhere and who need to set up some very basic cooking facilities in their apartments.

They have their dreams. They work hard, they would like to play hard too, but work related pressures are such that surviving on takeaways becomes the norm and sometimes even the preferred option. They, however, neither have the time nor the inclination to bother with anything but a very simple Survival Course in Cooking, which is what this book ventures to provide.

The third category could be that of the single moms or dads who suddenly realize the need to acquire some basic culinary skills FAST.

Finally, I address the needs of the small but growing tribe of campers, and those opting to stay in self-service apartments, while on tours and vacations, who too wish to acquire somewhat decent skills in cooking.

In short, this book is for anyone and everyone who wishes to learn about the magical art of cooking even if he or she has never boiled an egg before.

Research shows that manufactured food products contain harmful additives that are not really good for anybody. Pre-cooked and packaged foods also come loaded with hidden fat, sodium, and preservatives and on top of that keep on losing, whatever little nutrition they originally started with, in storage. It is becoming more and more important, therefore, to cook your own food no matter what circumstances you find yourselves in.

In this book, I share with you some very easy yet practical instructions that I used to jot down in my diary in my UCL days. These tricks and tips, from my mom, have really helped me in learning how to make meals from scratch. She would answer all my questions, doubts and fears, and encourage me to set me off on tasks such as how to boil an egg or chicken (a simple skill in cooking generally taken for granted).

I realized that many people, who are not able to master cooking, flounder because they cannot find anyone who could answer their simple or "stupid" questions (some people do after all consider how to boil an egg a stupid question!!). So, they just give up.

I hope the instructions that answered all my questions regarding cooking will answer yours as well. In this book, I am recounting my own personal experiences and mistakes so that you need not repeat the same. And yes, please be assured that there is nothing like a laughable question.

You may, if you so wish, start with such seemingly easy tasks as how to boil an egg, how to peel a boiled egg and how to break an egg for omelettes flawlessly.

And then, with the step-by-step graduation process that I describe, you can, just as I did, "graduate" to making egg sandwiches, sautéing vegetables, boiling chicken and much more.

Bon appetit then!

IV

WHY SHOULD YOU LEARN COOKING

Do we really need to discuss this?

Talking for me, I earnestly believe that cooking is as much of a life skill as is cycling, walking, jogging, swimming or writing. You ignore acquiring such a life skill at your own peril, don't you?

Cooking is an important aspect of your health and fitness regime and, therefore, (let me shock you) should very much be put on the same pedestal as working out. Cooking is also an education in itself. Just as a graduation in a particular subject gives you the foundation upon which your future career is built, cooking too prepares for you the base for a healthy lifestyle.

But leave aside the philosophy. Learning to cook from scratch, with fresh ingredients, can save you loads of money, in due course.

Just pick up any dish and first jot down its price in a restaurant, or even in a fast food joint. Next, calculate the price of all the ingredients of the same dish if you buy them from a supermarket and slap the whole dish together at your home. Despite the benefits of bulk buying and industrial scale processing, it will always be the latter strategy that will save you more money. And those savings can't hurt anyone, can they?

What about the time "wasted" on cooking at home? Well, let me assure you that if you internalize the tips and tricks shared in this Book's style of **Cooking In A Jiffy**, you will almost always be able to make your favourite dish in lesser time than what it will take you to go to a restaurant and order and eat your food.

How Only Home-Style Cooking Can Ensure Putting Nutritious Food on Your Table

Many celebrities and models in the glamorous world of films or fashion (where your survival depends on how your body looks) will tell you that 75% of your body is made in the kitchen and only 25% is due to workouts. By learning the art of cooking, you gain full control over this vital 75% by deciding what you eat, how much oil, salt and spices you put in your food, how many calories your food is allowed to contain, etc.

I have already highlighted that pre-packaged food contains harmful additives and preservatives that you can avoid only when you trust your own hands. Moreover, only by having your own food cooked under your own roof, can you ensure that you get proper intake of vitamins, minerals, trace elements, carbohydrates, proteins, fat and sugar.

Convinced? But not sure how complicated the whole process could be?

Let us then discuss how to go about setting up a very basic kitchen.

Lesson 1

HOW TO SET UP YOUR VERY BASIC KITCHEN

Absolute Essentials

Stove/Heat source: The first thing you would need in your kitchen would be a stove/heat source which could run on electricity or gas. If your kitchen is "bare" (as in many countries like India), you naturally have to first invest into this device.

At the simplest level, you may have to choose among a four burner, two burner or even a single burner model. The price difference between the various models may not be much but in my experience, it is always advisable to pick up at least a two stove version if you intend to cook a full meal. Otherwise for making simple one dish items, even a single stove should suffice.

A deep non-stick pan: You need this for sautéing vegetables, boiling/ poaching chicken and fish or even for boiling water.

Shallow non-stick pan: This is suggested as it is easier to make omelettes, scrambled egg, fried eggs in a shallow pan.

Grater: This is required for grating cheese and some vegetables which might require grating.

Two wooden spatulas for stirring and taking out the cooked stuff from the pan. Remember if you use a stainless steel one, you will scratch the non-stick/Teflon coating of the pan and spoil it.

Two sharp knives: Preferably in two different coloured handles, one for cutting vegetables, including onions and garlic, and a separate one for cutting fruits.

I am suggesting this because onions and garlic leave such a pungent smell that even after the knife has been washed, the smell can get transferred to the fruit or nuts you may be cutting for your dessert. Unless you love having your cut apples with a garlic smell (ha, ha)!!

A cutting board for cutting vegetables, fruits and anything else that might need chopping.

Two bowls for beating eggs, keeping cut vegetables, etc.

Crockery and Cutlery for serving and eating the food.

Optional As Your Needs Expand

Blender/Grinder: As your cooking skills improve, you may like to invest in this category to help you have dishes like smoothies, milk shakes, cold coffee, soups and also to make pastes of onion, garlic, ginger, etc.

Microwave cum oven: Needless to say but a microwave cum oven can expand your cooking horizon tremendously. Nothing can beat a microwave when it comes to re-heating food. For baking dishes too, you can use this appliance.

Do choose the "invertor" variety, if possible, for outstanding results. These not only allow you to do your bit towards the environment but are more efficient and also prove to be cheaper in the long run with lower electricity bills.

Pressure cooker: Though this device is not very popular in the west, in India, it is an absolute essential and helps you cook from curries to rice in a jiffy. If you are alone, a three litre (six US pints approximately) size is alright but if you are a family of three or four, then a five litre (eleven US pints approximately) size is suggested.

Wok: This Asian contraption is excellent for making a wide variety of dishes (especially Indian, Chinese or Thai) as the wide open mouth makes it very easy to stir or deep fry anything, with less oil too.

Refrigerator: This is absolutely essential for storing both cooked and fresh food. The freezer not only makes ice and preserves your ice cream but is essential for storing excess food which you may like to eat after a few days or even few weeks. It also can store frozen raw chicken, fish and meat saving you from making many unnecessary trips to the supermarket.

Once again, do choose the "invertor" variety, if possible, for outstanding performance and lower electricity bills.

Dish washer: This takes away the drudgery of cleaning up your dishes after you are done with the cooking and eating.

Rice maker: This contraption not only helps making rice idiot-proof but also keeps it hot and fluffy till you are ready to eat it.

Toaster: If you like to have hot toasts or heating waffles, then this should be one of the first appliances you should invest in.

Grill: If you like to have grilled sandwiches, chicken, fish, etc. then you may like to procure this device as well. In that case, you may like to review your decision to buy a toaster separately.

Electric kettle: This helps to boil water for making tea very quickly to enable you to make your tea/coffee/hot chocolate in a jiffy.

Coffee Machine: If you are a coffee-lover, then you would know a lot more than me about these bewildering array of machines. So go ahead and indulge yourself with whatever you can afford.

Lesson 2

WHAT INGREDIENTS YOU NEED TO STOCK AND EXPERIMENT WITH

At my Hall of Residence, I hardly stored anything. This was because we had common fridges which were most of the time quite cramped for space. Moreover, many people used to "borrow" (without permission, of course, if you know what I mean!) our items from these common fridges.

I still remember the calamity that befell me when I once bought a ready-to-eat Chicken Tikka Masala for my dinner. When I opened the fridge, after a long tiring day, with the intention to heat it, I realized that the chicken that I had so lovingly bought the very same morning had grown wings and disappeared.

Disappointing and disconcerting and hugely irritating as it was, this was nothing compared to the agony of those students who suddenly found their favourite (and rare) deer salamis bought from their home towns mysteriously disappearing overnight.

The lesson: if you stay in such "freely borrowable" conditions, don't overstock on anything. However, if you are staying all by yourself (or with a trusted friend or partner) and are privileged enough to have your own fridge, you may want to stock up on some frequently used ingredients that can be very useful for cooking.

A rough list is indicated below which is not exhaustive in any way. Please feel free to add your own ingredients that you think would be absolutely essential to prepare the kind of food that you long for.

Butter: This is a very versatile medium which adds a lot of flavour and aroma to the food you are cooking. Really helpful if you are making sauté vegetables or scrambling eggs.

Cooking Oil (of your preference; olive, soya, coconut, sesame, mustard...): Another basic requirement for making most vegetables, meats and seafood.

Salt: This is self-explanatory as most dishes would require a bit of salt to make them palatable.

Pepper: This should add a little zing to your food.

Sugar/Sugar substitute: This is required for making desserts as also for adding in other recipes to enhance their flavor.

Cheese-the kinds you like: These are easy to store and can make a lot of difference to the taste of many dishes. Cheddar Cheese is very helpful in making white sauce. Mozzarella can be used in baking and making cheese toasts. Parmesan can be sprinkled on to any dish to make it taste "cheesy"...

Tomato puree and Ketchup: Both of them add a lot of flavor to your dishes. Tomato puree can also be used as a cooking medium for many dishes. Ketchup is good for having with sandwiches.

Dijon Mustard: It is healthy and spices up your dish.

Mayonnaise: Helps making salads and sandwiches instantly. If you like low fat mayonnaise, then go for that.

Milk: A complete meal in itself. It can be consumed alone, with breakfast cereals or in making dishes like white sauce.

Wheat flour: I like the whole wheat variety as it is healthier than refined flour. Helps in making sauces and can be used in making many dishes.

Eggs: Versatility itself. Can be used to make a meal in a jiffy anytime, anywhere. Otherwise an egg is always suitable for a breakfast and keeps you full till lunch.

Fruits and Vegetables-frozen or fresh of your choice: Necessary to get essential vitamins and minerals and to keep you healthy and glowing.

Potatoes: Potatoes are of different kinds. You can buy baby potatoes to make sauté which goes well as a side dish with chicken/fish. You can also buy bigger potatoes to boil and mash them again for a good side dish.

Onion, Garlic & Ginger: Adding flavour and nutrition to your food.

Lemon: for giving a lemony flavour and tanginess to your grills and also for pepping up your food with its sourness.

Vinegar: Very good for marinating and for making poach eggs.

Dried Oregano, Rosemary, and other herbs: of your choice to sprinkle on your food

Breads of your choice

Region-specific spices:

For Indian dishes: Cumin seeds, turmeric, coriander powder, *Garam Masala* (mixture of green and brown cardamom, cinnamon, cloves, black pepper and bay leaves), etc.

For Chinese: Soya sauce, Chilli sauce, etc.

For Thai: Lemongrass, Galangal, Kafir lime etc.

.......I am sure you would know this list better.

Lesson 3

HOW TO MAKE TEA OR COFFEE

Tea

Teas come broadly in two types. One which come in sachets and the other which has to be brewed. This is true for all types of tea whether it is green, or black or flavour infused.

For newbies, it may be safe to pick up the sachet variety as it is easy to make and dispose of. We also suggest buying/using an electric kettle (with auto cut-off) as it takes out the suspense from when the water has properly boiled.

Method for making tea using sachets

In an electric kettle, or a deep sauce pan, place a mug of water (or as much as you need) for boiling.

When the water comes to a boil, pour the water into the mug and dip the sachet into it @one sachet per cup.

Let the tea brew for about 2 minutes.

Remove the sachet (twirl it around a spoon to take out all the liquor if you like your tea to be strong) and your tea is ready.

In case, you like to have your tea with milk and sugar, then after you remove the sachet, add a tablespoon or two of milk as per your liking and add the sugar too.

Stir well and enjoy your sweet milky tea.

Method for brewing your tea-the Classic Darjeeling way

In case you like to brew your tea, then measure out one teaspoon for every cup/mug you want to make and add one more for the tea pot.

Place the tea leaves in a ceramic pot (preferably) and after the water boils, pour the boiling water over the leaves.

Cover the pot so that it remains warm and let it brew for 5 minutes.

Thereafter strain the liquid into a mug and your tea is ready.

In case, you like to have your tea with milk and sugar, then after you remove the tea leaves, add a tablespoon or two of milk as per your liking and add the sugar too.

Stir well and enjoy your sweet milky tea.

Tip: The left over tea leaves make for excellent fertilizer for such plants as rose bushes. So if you do have these bushes nearby, remember to bury your used tea leaves near their roots instead of trashing them unnecessarily.

Coffee

The simplest coffee to make is the instant variety. For this you need to buy instant coffee powder for any type of coffee that you like, be it Costa Rican, Columbian, Brazilian, Kenyan or any other variety.

In a mug, put 1 teaspoon of coffee.

Boil a mug of water in the electric kettle or deep sauce pan.

When the water boils, pour the same onto the coffee.

You should leave some place in the mug if you want to add milk and sugar or you can fill it up if you want to have it black.

You can also have your coffee without water but with hot or cold milk. That's actually the way I like it with my breakfast which helps me get a caffeine kick with some added calcium and protein.

Lesson 4

HOW TO TOAST BREAD AND GRADUATE TO MAKING BREAD CRUMBS, GARLIC TOASTS AND CHEESE GARLIC TOASTS

How to Make Toast

For making a good toast, you will need to have a toaster (or grill or oven) and sliced bread of your choice that is white, brown, multigrain etc.

Place the bread in the toaster and press the toaster to start. Most toasters have dials to indicate the degree to which you want the toast to brown. Choose your setting and if it is a pop up toaster, your toast will come out automatically when done.

In case it is not, then you will have to watch to see that your toast has browned properly and then press the off button to take out your toast.

How to Make Bread Crumbs

Bread crumbs can prove to be useful when you are confident enough to experiment with making KFC style chicken or fish at home.

For making bread crumbs, you can take some left over bread which is already a little hard. Toast it well in the toaster. Take it out and let it cool down a bit. Take a spatula and beat the toast till it all turns into crumbs.

You can make and store these crumbs at leisure whenever you have some left over bread. This will save a lot of time when you want to make another dish requiring bread crumbs.

How to Make Garlic Toast

Ingredients

Bread-2 slices preferably cut thick (you can use any bread, or even bun of your choice)

Garlic-5 cloves crushed

Salted Butter-20 grams (1oz) (1 tablespoon)

Any fresh green herb of choice

Method

In a pan, warm up the butter and add the crushed garlic.

Let it cook for a minute and then switch off.

Meanwhile, toast the bread (or bun) well.

Spread the garlic mixture on the toast.

You can sprinkle any fresh herbs on this toast.

Your delicious garlic bread is ready.

How to Make a Cheese Garlic Toast

Ingredients

Bread-2 slices preferably cut thick (you can use any bread, or even bun of your choice)

Garlic-5 cloves crushed

Salted Butter-20 grams (0.70oz) (1 tablespoon)

Grated Cheddar Cheese-25 grams (0.88oz) (1 + 1/2 tablespoon)

Any fresh green herb of choice

Method

In a pan, warm up the butter and add the crushed garlic.

Let it cook for a minute and then add the grated cheese.

Let the cheese melt.

Meanwhile, toast the bread (or bun) well.

Spread this mixture on the toast.

You can sprinkle any fresh herbs on this toast.

Your delicious cheese garlic toast is ready.

Lesson 5

HOW TO BOIL AND PEEL AN EGG FLAWLESSLY AND GRADUATE TO DO MUCH MORE

Now we should take up some really serious cooking.

Why Should You Learn to Boil an Egg

For an absolute newbie, learning how to boil an egg should definitely be the first port of call. When I too learnt to boil an egg at my Hall of Residence, it boosted my self-confidence like nothing could. I could now have a complete breakfast consisting of a boiled egg along with some cereals that I bought from the supermarket and a glass of cold milk. I felt really proud that I could make myself a simple breakfast without any help and without "wasting" even five minutes. This eventually opened my eyes for further experimentation.

Boiling an egg also proved to be a foundation for many more recipes. Once I knew how to boil an egg, I could make myself an egg sandwich. When my confidence grew even more, I could experiment with making other egg recipes such as a scrambled egg, egg poach or even an egg fry.

I hope mastering the art of boiling an egg (which is hardly an art) would give you the same amount of pleasure and assurance that it gave me and would encourage you to try out making many other egg recipes.

My first experience with boiling an egg

On a foggy Sunday morning, and bored with my usual cold breakfast of cereals and milk, I decided to experiment with boiling an egg. I had never boiled an egg before in my entire life and the feeling of trying something new did unnerve me a little. So, I first spoke to my mom over Skype and carefully scribbled down some tips.

The first tip, which I was not aware of, was to take out the egg from the fridge and to let it come to room temperature. This is because the egg is really cold when it is taken out of the fridge. When the same egg is put in water, and the process of boiling starts, a sudden temperature difference created between the egg and the water can sometimes lead to the egg cracking up inside the pot.

The second tip was that I should put water first in the pan and then let the egg slip in. If I did the other way around, there could be a possibility of the egg rolling around and breaking in the pan while I clumsily took the pan with egg to the washbasin to add water.

As instructed, therefore, I first let the egg come to room temperature. Then I filled the pot with water which was enough for the egg to be submerged. After that I carefully placed the egg inside the water, put the pan on the hot plate and then switched it on.

For a few seconds, it looked like nothing had happened. I was alarmed enough to place my hands near the pan to check if it was heating up. Slowly I could see the water shaking as if there was a mild earthquake. Small bubbles soon started forming at the bottom of the pot which in a few more seconds turned into bigger and bigger and bigger bubbles. At this point, I realized that the water was coming to a boil.

As soon as the water came to a boil, I was instructed to turn off the heat source and let the water cool down on its own. I could only then remove the egg from the water.

Voila, my idiot-proof hard-boiled egg was ready.

Personally I don't like half boiled or semi-boiled egg. So I never experimented with these. But in case you are fond of them, my mom suggests to remove the egg the moment the water comes to a boil (and NOT wait till the water cools down on its own).

How Should You Then Boil an Egg

To recapitulate I would suggest the following steps to boil an egg:

Take out the egg from the fridge and let it come to room temperature.

In a pot, take enough water for the egg to be fully submerged.

Add the egg and then turn on the heat source.

As soon as the water comes to a boil, turn off the heat source and let the water cool down on its own.

Remove the egg from the water.

Remove the shell. Your perfect hard-boiled egg is ready.

In case, you want to have a half boiled or a semi boiled egg, then unlike in a hard-boiled egg where you remove the egg from the water after letting the water come to room temperature from its boiling point, it is suggested to remove the egg the moment the water comes to a boil.

How Should You Peel a Perfect Boiled Egg

After you have boiled the egg, and taken it out of the boiling water, immerse it in cold water for a minute. This helps you to handle the egg easily and also loosens the shell. Thereafter, gently tap the upper pointed portion of the egg with a fork till small cracks appear. Now start peeling from this point and the shell should come out easily if the egg is full boiled.

Tip: In case, you find the shell sticking at places, you can break the egg at a few more places with the fork, and then roll the entire egg in your palm for a few seconds to loosen the shell.

For half boiled egg, take out only the upper portion to the point where you can dip a small spoon inside the egg-shell. Then place the egg in an egg bowl and scoop out the egg with a spoon to eat.

Congratulations, you have just completed your first **Cooking In a Jiffy** lesson of how to boil and peel a perfect egg.

Graduate Now to Making an Egg Sandwich

Once you have learnt to boil an egg, you can easily progress to making this simple sandwich. This is what I used to do in my London Hall of Residence to save me from the torture of consuming tasteless, and "plasticky" egg sandwiches from the supermarket. Besides saving me some money, this dish boosted my confidence like nothing could, and I sincerely believe that it will do the same to you.

Ingredients

Hard Boiled egg-1

Mayonnaise-1 level tablespoon

Dijon Mustard-1/4 teaspoon

A pinch of salt

Powdered sugar-1/4 teaspoon

Bread-2 slices (of your choice)

Lettuce, tomatoes, cucumber or any other such filler/salad of your choice-Optional

Method

Boil the egg the same way that you have learnt. This is how you should boil an egg:

Take out the egg from the fridge and let it come to room temperature.

In a pot, take enough water for the egg to be fully submerged.

Add the egg and then turn on the heat source.

As soon as the water comes to a boil, turn off the heat source and let the water cool down on its own.

Remove the egg from the water.

Remove the shell. Your perfect hard-boiled egg is ready.

Mash the egg well with fork and then put in the mayonnaise and Dijon Mustard and mix well.

Now, sprinkle a pinch of salt and the powdered sugar and again mix well.

Spread this mixture on to a slice of bread.

Put salad/filler of your choice. Cover with another slice of bread and cut into two triangles. Your delicious Jiffy Egg Sandwich is ready.

Prep time: 5 minutes

Cooking time: 5 minutes (for the egg to boil and for you to peel it)

Total time: 10 minutes

Making Grilled Egg Sandwich

After making my own egg sandwiches, I now wanted to experiment with the preparation of a nice warm grilled egg sandwich. I had always loved grilled sandwiches, with those nice grill lines, which not only looked good but also tasted divine.

My mom's grilled egg sandwiches used to have an egg filling with grated cheese and mustard paste that could keep me full till lunch. This meant that I had fewer hunger pangs and, therefore, didn't need to snack in between.

So I first bought a bottle of Dijon Mustard, some onions and some tomatoes. I grated the cheese and chopped my onions and tomatoes. In parallel, I boiled (and peeled) an egg and then mashed it in a bowl. I mixed this with all other ingredients. Then I spread the mixture gently on one slice of the bread and pressed it with another slice of bread to make a sandwich.

My mom had told me to put the sandwich on a cold grill (not a pre-heated grill) and then to switch the grill on. This is because this helps in slowly browning the sandwich better. I was also instructed to keep checking the grill to see that the sandwich had reached the desired level of brownness. Once I realized that the sandwich had become crisp brown, I switched off the grill and took out my perfectly grilled egg sandwich to admire and devour.

The sandwich was certainly not as good as my mom's. I could have probably chopped the onion and tomatoes finer but anyways I felt really proud of the fact that I could now grill a sandwich at my Hall of Residence and didn't need to visit a deli for this warm sandwich.

There is no reason why you couldn't "graduate" the same way. Once you are confident with boiling an egg and making a simple egg sandwich, graduating to a grilled egg sandwich does not look daunting anymore. Please don't worry if in your first attempt you were not able to chop onions and tomatoes that well or that you "overbrowned" or "under browned" (if such a term exists) your grilled sandwich. The most important thing is to make an attempt and to learn from your mistakes. The more you will practice, the better you will get at it. Be proud of the fact that you can now have something warm for yourself for your meals apart from that hot coffee from your nearest deli.

Here is then the full set of instructions which should help you too accomplish this mission as breezily as I could.

Ingredients

Egg-1 Hard boiled and shelled

Grated Cheese-25 grams (1oz) (1 + 1/2 tablespoon)

Butter-1 teaspoon

Tomato Ketchup-2 teaspoon

English/Dijon Mustard paste-1/4 teaspoon

Chopped up onion-1 teaspoon

Chopped up tomatoes-1 teaspoon

Bread-2 slices (of your choice)

A pinch of Salt and Pepper

Tip: Did you notice that I have NOT included mayonnaise (which I did for the simple egg sandwich) in the above list? This is so because mayo, when heated up in a grill, leads to the separation of its oil base that then tastes awful!

Method

Boil an egg the way you have learnt. This is how you should boil an egg:

Take out the egg from the fridge and let it come to room temperature.

In a pot, take enough water for the egg to be fully submerged.

Add the egg and then turn on the heat source.

As soon as the water comes to a boil, turn off the heat source and let the water cool down on its own.

Remove the egg from the water.

Remove the shell. Your perfect hard-boiled egg is ready.

In a bowl, mash your hardboiled egg well till the egg looks like a mashed potato.

Add together all other ingredients and mix well.

Spread on one piece of bread and press the other slice to make a sandwich.

Put this sandwich into a COLD (not preheated) grill, close cover, and switch it on.

Let the sandwich become crisp slowly.

A good idea is to have a peek inside the grill, once in a while, to check if the toast has reached the desired level of brownness.

Take the sandwich out on to a plate.

You may like to cut your grilled egg sandwich in half, diagonally, to make it easier to eat.

Prep time: 5 minutes

Cooking time: 5 minutes

Total time: 10 minutes

Note: Please note that this recipe is for one egg and for one person. If you are making a grilled egg sandwich for more eggs, then you need to multiply all the ingredients in equal proportion.

Making Scrambled Egg

I had always wondered why the scrambled egg served in my Hall of Residence looked, felt and tasted "rubbery" whereas the one made in my home was so creamy that I needed a spoon, rather than the usual fork, to relish it. What could be the possible secret? My mom explained that just adding a little milk and cheese to the scrambled egg makes all the difference.

So on a Sunday morning at my Hall of Residence, I gathered courage to try making scrambled eggs the way they should be made. As taught, in a non-stick pan, I broke an egg by gently tapping the upper portion of the egg with a fork till I could see a crack appearing. I kept tapping that portion of the egg till the crack turned into a small hole big enough for the egg to be poured out on to the non-stick pan. One needs to be gentle here and should try not to tap the egg so hard that the entire egg breaks all of a sudden in your hand, either spoiling your clothes or dropping on the floor.

What I really like about the scrambled egg is that there is no need to either separate the egg yolk from the egg white (needed for fluffy omelettes) or to ensure that the egg yolk remains intact (needed for egg fry or egg poach). So even if you happened to break the egg in such a way that the egg yolk broke and mixed with the egg white, it will not make any difference to the quality of your scrambled egg.

After that, I scooped a tablespoon of butter, added a tablespoon of milk, grated cheese, a pinch of salt and pepper and put all of the ingredients in the pan where I mixed them all well. Then I put the pan on my hotplate and switched on. I was instructed to immediately reduce the heat to medium, and to stir the mixture continuously. I struggled a bit with the stirring realizing that my stirring was not as effective as my mom's. I had to ensure that the mixture did not stick to the pan or get burnt.

As soon as the mixture thickened, I switched off the heat source and while stirring continuously, poured the mixture onto a serving plate. This was the first time I made for myself a scrambled egg. It was far from perfect. While breaking the egg, by mistake, some egg shells had gone into the pan, which I realized only when I could sense the crunchiness of the egg shells in the scrambled egg. My stirring could have been better and I could have made the egg a little thicker.

With practice my scrambled eggs had to become better. I was also now diligent enough to not break the egg in such a way that egg shells fell into the pan. My stirring had improved and with gradual practice even the consistency improved. At last, my scrambled eggs became creamier just the way they were at my home.

I am narrating all this to convey that if you mess up, you are not alone. Also any such setback shouldn't deter you from experimenting. So please keep practicing till you get a hold of things and one day I can assure you that your friends too will be praising you for making scrambled eggs that are better than whatever they can find in any professional restaurant.

Let me then recapitulate some tips and tricks, and do's and don'ts to successfully create this version of the scrambled egg.

Note: This recipe is for one egg. In case you need to make more, just multiply all ingredients, in equal proportion.

Ingredients

Egg-1

Milk-1 tablespoon

Butter-1 teaspoon

Grated Cheese-1 tablespoon

Salt and Pepper-Just a sprinkle

Method

Over a non-stick pan, gently tap the upper portion of an egg to make a small hole for you to pour the liquid in the pan comfortably. Please be careful and ensure that no portion of the egg shell goes into the pan. There is no need to separate the egg yolk from the egg white.

Now put the rest of the ingredients in and mix it all well.

Put the pan on your cook stove and switch on the heat source. Immediately reduce the heat to medium.

Stir the mixture continuously ensuring that the mixture neither STICKS TO THE PAN NOR BURNS.

As soon as the mixture cooks (that is when there is no liquid left), switch off the heat source and while stirring continuously, pour the mixture onto a serving plate.

Remember if the mixture becomes too dry or lumpy, it will no longer taste creamy and if the mixture remains too wet, it will give a raw taste.

Tip: A common pitfall is to add more milk than suggested or to forget to put the milk altogether. In both cases, the scrambled egg will NOT taste as good as we want it to be. Another pitfall is to add a lot of salt. This recipe requires just a pinch of salt and pepper because butter and cheese already contain some salt.

Prep time: 3 minutes

Cooking time: 2 minutes

Total time: 5 minutes

Making an Egg Fry

I am not a great fan of egg fries myself. So let me admit that I never tried making these at my Hall of Residence. My mom, however, differs. For her, nothing can be faster than adding a crisp egg fry, sunny side up, and with all the goodness of the first class protein, zinc and other nutrients that eggs contain, to your breakfast.

I had seen a girl in my Hall of Residence struggling to make egg fries. Sometimes her egg yolk would break. The resultant mess didn't inspire me enough to try my hand at making egg fries myself. However, my curiosity was pricked enough to ask my mom about how could one ever create a perfect egg fry.

The objective was to have a set, or congealed, egg white on the periphery with the liquidy and delicious egg yolk in the middle that remains unbroken till you put your spoon to it.

This is what I learnt then.

Tip: In case you need to fry more than one egg, all sunny side up, please do it one at a time.

Ingredients

Egg-1

Cooking Oil/Butter-1 tablespoon

A pinch of salt and pepper

Method

Take a non-stick frying pan and add the butter or the cooking oil.

Fire up the heat source and let the cooking oil warm up.

Meanwhile, gently break the egg in a small bowl carefully ensuring that no portion of the egg shell goes into the bowl. Unlike what we did for the scrambled egg recipe, here you will need to tap the middle of the egg with a fork till a crack appears. Keep tapping till the crack becomes bigger and you can then comfortably break the egg into two halves pouring all the liquid in the bowl. PLEASE TRY NOT TO BREAK THE YOLK OF THE EGG.

Add the egg to the oil and let it sizzle.

As soon as the egg white sets, carefully take it out on a plate.

Sprinkle a little bit of salt and pepper.

Your single fried egg, sunny side up, is ready.

Note: If you like "double fry" eggs, then after the last stage, just flip the egg down and let the sunny side touch the pan for a minute and become firm.

Prep time: 1 min

Cooking time: 2 minutes

Total time: 3 minutes

Some people may find making an egg fry easier as it does not require continuous stirring as in a scrambled egg. However, the breaking part of the egg could be trickier and requires a little practice.

Making Egg Poach

If you like egg fry but wish to reduce its calories (or greasiness), then this oil-free egg poach recipe could be your best option. Yes, you heard it right, this egg dish requires NO butter or cooking oil and still tastes as good as a "normal" egg fry. Ok, make it almost as good....

Conceptually you may find poaching an egg easier than making an egg fry.

Note: The pan size you select for this recipe will depend on the number of eggs you want to poach at a time; that is a bigger pan will be required for more eggs, maximum four at a time.

Note: The recipe given here is for one egg. In case you need to make more, you should normally just multiply all ingredients, in equal proportion. However, PLEASE DON'T INCREASE THE QUANTITY OF VINEGAR TO MORE THAN 1 TEASPOON, OTHERWISE IT WILL ADD A VERY SOUR TASTE TO THE EGG. BUT DO INCREASE THE AMOUNT OF WATER PROPORTIONATELY.

Ingredients

Egg-1

Water-1 cup

Vinegar-1/4 teaspoon

Salt-1/4 teaspoon

Method

In a small pan, pour the water and bring it to a boil.

Add the vinegar and salt.

Break the egg in a small bowl the same way you did for the egg fry. To recapitulate, you will first need to tap the middle of the egg with a fork till a crack appears. Keep tapping till the crack becomes bigger and you can then comfortably break the egg into two neat halves pouring all the liquid in the bowl .PLEASE MAKE SURE THAT YOU DON'T BREAK THE YOLK OF THE EGG.

Gently pour the egg into the pan.

Both the egg white and yolk will soon set.

Gently take the egg out of the water and put it in a plate.

Your poached egg is ready.

Prep time: 2 minutes

Cooking time: 3 minutes

Total time: 5 minutes

Making Basic Omelette

If you are fond of omelettes, we suggest you use this recipe to practice making them. You should certainly try this simple recipe out before graduating to making cheese omelettes or any other advanced versions of omelettes.

Ingredients

Eggs-2

Salt and pepper to taste

Cooking Oil/Butter-1 tablespoon

Method

In a bowl break the eggs. You will need to tap the middle of the egg with a fork till a crack appears. Keep tapping till the crack becomes bigger. You can then comfortably break the egg into two halves pouring all the liquid in the bowl without bothering if in the process the egg yolk breaks or not.

Beat the egg well with a fork and add the salt and pepper to taste.

In a non-stick shallow pan, heat the butter/cooking oil. Gently roll the pan to coat the entire pan with the cooking medium.

Now pour the batter to the pan and reduce the heat to minimum.

Gently roll the pan so that the egg batter covers the whole pan and let the egg cook.

When the egg looks cooked, that is when the egg is set and there are no traces of liquid, gently fold the egg in half and remove from the heat.

Cover a plate with a paper napkin and turn the omelette on to the same. The paper napkin will absorb all excess oil.

Remove the paper napkin and enjoy your basic omelette

Prep time: 5 minutes

Cooking time: 3 minutes

Total time: 8 minutes

Making Cheese Omelette

This cheese omelette recipe is an all-time favourite that can be part of any meal, any time of the day, or night.

Many a times we were served cheese omelette for dinner in our Hall of Residence. Personally, I was happy with my scrambled egg and grilled sandwiches. But quite a few people at my Hall of Residence did enjoy making cheese omelettes.

So here is my version.

Please note that you should graduate to making cheese omelettes only if you are confident with the process of making a simple omelette. The good news is that the two recipes are very similar and once you have learnt to make a basic omelette, you can very easily make a cheese omelette.

Ingredients

Eggs-2

Cheese Slice-2

Butter/Cooking Oil-1 tablespoon

Salt and pepper to taste

Tip: Keep salt to the minimum as cheese and butter too contain some salt.

Method

In a bowl break the eggs. You will need to tap the middle of the egg with a fork till a crack appears. Keep tapping till the crack becomes bigger and you can then comfortably break the egg into two halves pouring all the liquid in the bowl.

Beat the egg well with a fork and add the salt and pepper to taste.

In a non-stick shallow pan, heat the butter/cooking oil. Gently roll the pan to coat the entire pan with the cooking medium.

Now pour the batter to the pan and reduce the heat to minimum.

Gently roll the pan so that the egg batter covers the whole pan and let the egg cook.

When the egg looks cooked, that is when the egg is set and there are no traces of liquid, place the cheese slices on the egg.

Gently fold the egg in half and immediately remove from the heat.

Cover a plate with a paper napkin and turn the omelette on to the same. The paper napkin will absorb all excess oil.

Remove the paper napkin and enjoy your delicious cheese omelette.

Note: Since the cheese will melt inside this folded omelette, it is highly recommended that you eat it piping hot.

Prep time: 5 minutes

Cooking time: 3 minutes

Total time: 8 minutes

Making Dad's Spicy French Toast Salted (!)

Whether you like it sweet or salted, French toast is usually quite a favourite in any part of the world. In England, at my Hall of Residence, however, when French toasts were served on Fridays, hardly any one liked it. We all found it smelly, greasy and quite unappetizing.

But when my mom makes French toast, it always tasted divine. I asked my mom about the secret ingredient.

Can you guess what that is?

It is butter (and not cooking oil). Butter is the ingredient that imparts a really nice flavour. However, if you don't like the "buttery" taste, please feel free to use any cooking oil which you prefer or are familiar with.

To make your French toast less greasy, we suggest that after browning you use a paper napkin to absorb all the excess oil. Please see the method below to see how you can exactly do it.

I remember having French toast at home occasionally. My father is actually so fond of them that he sometimes "decorates" them with Thai chilli sauce, a teaspoon of chopped tomatoes, onion and coriander.

Note: This recipe is for one egg. In case you need to make more, just multiply all ingredients, in equal proportion.

Ingredients

Egg-1

Bread slices-2

Milk-4 tablespoon

Salt and pepper to taste

Butter-2 tablespoon

Optional

Chopped Onion- 1 table spoon

Chopped Tomato- 1 table spoon

Fresh Coriander (or any green herb of your choice) chopped-1 table spoon

Method

In a bowl, gently break the egg, ensuring that no portion of the egg shell goes into the bowl.

Whisk the egg well and add the milk, the salt and pepper.

In a pan, add the butter. You will see that the butter starts melting slowly.

As the butter is "warming up", dip a slice of bread in the batter and let it absorb some of it. PLEASE REMEMBER THAT IF YOU LET THE BREAD REMAIN IN THE BATTER FOR TOO LONG, IT WILL DISINTEGRATE.

Put the slice in the pan and gently brown it on both sides.

Remove to a serving dish which already has a paper napkin to absorb the excess oil/butter, if you so wish.

Do the same thing with the next slice. The batter should be just enough for two slices of bread.

Enjoy your French toast.

Optional: You may also "decorate" your exotic French toast with Thai Chilli sauce, chopped tomatoes, onions, coriander or any other herbs of your choice, as my father likes it.

Prep time: 5 minutes

Cooking time: 4 minutes @2 minutes each slice

Total time: 9 minutes

Making Sweet French Toast

If you like the conventionally sweet version of the French Toast, here is the recipe.

Ingredients

Egg-1

Bread slices-2

Milk-4 tablespoon

Powdered sugar-1 tablespoon

Salted Butter-2 tablespoon (this enhances the sweet taste)

Method

In a bowl, gently break the egg, ensuring that no portion of the egg shell goes into the bowl.

Whisk the egg well and add the milk, and the sugar.

In a pan, add the butter.

As the butter is "warming up", dip a slice of bread in the batter and let it absorb some of it. PLEASE REMEMBER THAT IF YOU LET THE BREAD REMAIN IN THE BATTER FOR TOO LONG, IT WILL DISINTEGRATE.

Put the slice in the pan and gently brown it on both sides.

Remove to a serving dish which already has a paper napkin to absorb the excess oil/butter, if you so wish.

Do the same thing with the next slice. The batter should be just enough for two slices of bread.

Enjoy your Sweet French toast.

Optional: You may like to have your Sweet French toast with honey or Maple Syrup, if you so desire.

Prep time: 5 minutes

Cooking time: 4 minutes @2 minutes each slice

Total time: 9 minutes

Conclusion

First of all I must congratulate you for having learnt how to break, boil, and peel an egg and do much more with it. You have indeed acquired a very valuable skill and what I would call as the foundation stone of cooking.

Please do not get upset if you had difficulties in replicating some recipes. The most important thing in life is to make an effort and the same goes for cooking. Most people would not even reach this stage. I have known countless number of people who have simply survived on instant noodles throughout their college years. (Yes, I have spoken to students residing by themselves, in India, who survived on a particular brand of instant noodles simply because it did not require to be boiled like other conventional noodles. You could simply tear open the packet and have it straightaway. Don't believe it, email me and I'll tell you the brand name.)

The net result is that your body suffers from a lack of nutrition and sooner than later you develop health problems. I have come across many colleagues who skip their breakfast to reach office on time and then survive on coffee, which too made from machines in their office! The most important reason is that most people nowadays in the industrialized world do not even know how to boil an egg, let alone make a proper breakfast.

When I had learnt to boil an egg, I felt so proud of the fact that I could have a decent breakfast that too cooked by myself. I felt very independent and liberated and so would you. So what if you could not break the eggs properly or your stirring was not effective like mine or that you accidentally dropped a few egg shells in the bowl in an attempt to break an egg. You should not be afraid of making mistakes. Only by learning from your mistakes, will you improve. I can guarantee you that nobody was born with cooking skills (when I say nobody, I mean your mom, grand mom or anyone else in your family). People simply acquire these skill-sets over time and yet continue to learn and make mistakes.

Instead of being daunted by failure, I suggest you awaken your adventurous spirit. I know that all of us have an adventurous spirit inside ourselves. People go for hiking, bungee jumping, river rafting, etc and I must tell you that cooking is not any different. Cooking is an invaluable skill which will remain with you for the rest of your life.

Let me tell you that when I started cooking, I too had similar fears. I feared that the egg will remain raw or I will burn myself or that the pot will explode due to overheating. I had to learn to put aside all these (rational or irrational) fears, and rekindle my adventurous spirit. That spirit that told me to do something new, to acquire a new skill, to experiment and not to think about failures. And I am sure, that you can also do the same thing.

Let the pleasure of cooking your own meals then overjoy you.

Lesson 6

HOW TO COOK YOUR VEGETABLES

Trust me, nobody can tell you better than myself that eating vegetables is important. The goodness, that green veggies come packed with, needs no introduction. Vitamins, minerals, beta carotene, lycopene---- think of any nutrient that your body needs and sure some vegetable can supply that.

I suffered personally for not making vegetable dishes for myself in the First term of my UCL days. I have already mentioned that when I came back to India in the winter of 2005, my friends and family members were shocked to find me looking so thin and pale. My mom forced me to take a pan to cook vegetables which I carried to London a little reluctantly.

The pan, however, proved to be an incentive for me to start experimenting with cooking vegetables in my second term. I started with sautéing peas, then moved to sautéing different vegetables one by one. I learnt that different vegetables take different time to cook. Finally, when I became confident enough I could sauté mixed vegetables.

This chapter also follows the same pattern. The best thing about sauté is that it does not require any technical skill but is extremely useful in learning and understanding the basics in cooking. You will learn to first sauté peas then move to making grilled tomatoes, sauté spinach, sauté mushrooms, roast baby potatoes, sauté mixed vegetables and finally experiment with tastier and more complicated dishes.

I would, however, advise you to wash your vegetables thoroughly if it is not canned or frozen. This should be done to ensure hygiene. Supermarkets, these days, also sell pre-cut and nicely packaged vegetables. Go for them and you would save a lot of time cutting vegetables yourself, especially if your cutting skills be as bad as mine when I had started learning how to cook.

Making Sauté peas

Many supermarkets nowadays sell packaged shelled peas or frozen peas. Go for this option to save a lot of your time. Otherwise you will have to shell peas manually which is time consuming and generates a lot of waste. Some people have asked me whether frozen peas, canned peas, packaged shelled peas or fresh peas taste any different. The answer is NO --there is no difference in taste. So feel free to use any kind of peas that you like.

I started my experiment with peas because I used to have them for breakfast. I also thought they were the simplest to make. In any case, it is always better to experiment with one vegetable and thoroughly understand its cooking time before moving on to another.

Ingredients

Peas Shelled-200 grams (7oz) (1 cup)

Butter-1 teaspoon

Water-2 tablespoon

Salt to taste

Method

Wash the peas thoroughly.

Light the fire and put the pan on it.

Add the butter and let it melt.

Add the peas and stir it well.

When the peas start changing colour (which is what I call magic!), add the salt.

Reduce the heat to minimum (SIM on a gas stove), add the water and cover the pan.

You will see that the steam starts escaping after a while.

Keep checking till the water dries up.

Tip: Please ensure that your peas don't burn or become mushy. You may also use a fork to poke the peas to ensure that it has been cooked properly. If the peas are tender, that means they have been cooked well.

Your sauté peas are ready.

Prep time: 2 minutes

Cooking time: 7-10 minutes

Total time: 9-11 minutes

Making Grilled tomatoes

At Ifor Evans, we were served grilled tomatoes for breakfast. This was a side dish with regular sausages, bacon, fried egg and a croissant. So when I learnt to grill tomatoes myself, I was excited that I could now make myself a proper breakfast even during the weekends. Add grilled tomatoes and sauté peas to your regular boiled egg or scrambled egg and you too can enjoy a proper breakfast. Mind you, grilling tomatoes is not at all difficult and there are very few chances for you going wrong.

Ingredients

Tomato-1 cut in half

Butter-1/2 teaspoon

Salt and Pepper to taste

Method

Wash the tomato thoroughly before cutting.

Cut the tomato in half.

Switch on your heat source and put a pan on it.

Add the butter and let it melt.

Place the tomato cut side down and let it sizzle for a minute.

Turn it around and give it another minute.

Put it on to a plate and sprinkle salt and pepper.

Your grilled tomato is ready.

Prep time: 2 minutes

Cooking time: 1-2 minutes

Total time: 3-4 minutes

Making Sauté baby potatoes

We used to be served baby potatoes with roast chicken. When I learnt to sauté baby potatoes, I was happy that I could make baby potatoes in the same way it was served in my Hall of Residence. You too can sauté baby potatoes exactly as you have been learning to sauté other vegetables.

Potatoes do have a rather bad-boy reputation of being full of sinful carbs. But if you still love the taste of potatoes, but are scared of the additional calories that its most popular avatar the French Fries come loaded with, then this simple dish which uses minimum oil is perfect for you. We suggest that you retain the potato's skin to benefit from the little vitamins and minerals that it comes packed with.

Ingredients

Baby Potatoes-250 grams (9oz) (1 cup)

Butter-25 grams (1oz) (1 + 1/2 tablespoon)

Water-half cup

Fresh herbs like Thyme or Rosemary

Salt and pepper to taste

Method

Wash the baby potatoes well and wherever needed cut them into half.

Switch on your heat source and put a pan on it.

Add the butter to the pan and let it melt.

Add the baby potatoes and stir well.

When the baby potatoes start changing colour, add a sprinkle of salt and keep stirring.

Reduce the heat to minimum (SIM on a gas stove), add the water and cover the pan.

You will see that the steam starts escaping after a while.

Keep checking till the water has dried.

Tip: You may also use a fork to poke the baby potatoes to ensure that they have been cooked properly. If the potatoes are tender that means they have been cooked well.

Your sauté baby potatoes are ready. You may add some pepper or your favourite herb like Rosemary or Thyme to make it more flavourful.

Prep time: 5 minutes

Cooking time: 10 minutes

Total time: 15 minutes

Making Spinach with butter

Spinach was my favourite veggie when I was a child and continues to remain a favourite till this day. I always enjoyed watching Popeye build bulging biceps after having canned spinach. After trying my hands on sauté peas and grilled tomatoes, I had now become confident enough to try out spinach. I must admit that I found spinach to be the most mystical of all the vegetables that I tried. When I bought a 500 gram packet of spinach from the supermarket, I was rather surprised to find that raw spinach looked like the leaves of some tree. This was the first time I had seen raw spinach. When I cooked spinach, I realized that spinach leaves a lot of water and a 500 gram packet which I thought was too much, was reduced to a serving size that was barely enough for one person.

If you hate spinach but love Popeye---then you too must try this simple spinach dish with butter. Easy to cook and full of nutrition, this green wonder recipe uses no spices.

Ingredients

Spinach (leaves only)-1 kg (approximately 2lb) (4 cups)

Butter-1 tablespoon

Salt to taste

Method

Wash the spinach thoroughly.

Switch on your heat source and put a pan on it.

Add the butter to the pan.

As soon as the butter melts, add the spinach and stir well.

Reduce the heat to minimum (SIM on a gas stove), and cover the pan.

The spinach will cook in its own juice.

When the spinach is fully cooked, add the salt.

If you like your spinach dry, then increase the heat and dry the spinach.

Tip: Please note that you don't need to add water, unlike for peas or any other vegetable. This is because spinach leaves a lot of water and can be cooked in its own juice.

Your green vegetable is ready in a jiffy. Once you become confident with making this dish, you may also try to add some cheese and cream to make it tastier. I experimented with goat brie cheese and it turned out to be really tasty.

If you wish to benefit from the heart-friendly goodness of garlic (and don't mind the smell that will linger on your hands and knife for quite some time) try out the Spinach with garlic variation. In this, you just need to add 4 cloves of chopped garlic at the stage where the butter has melted. Let these cook for a minute and then add the spinach.

Preparation time: 5 minutes

Cooking time: 10 minutes

Total: 15 minutes

Making Sauté Mixed Vegetables

If you have mastered the basics of sautéing peas, tomatoes or spinach, then graduating to sautéing mixed vegetables is a natural step. You could begin with buying pre-cut and cleaned vegetables from the supermarket, just to save on time. There were some really good collection of chopped carrots, cauliflower, broccoli, mushrooms, etc that I could readily find on the shelves.

The fascinating thing I find about sauté mixed vegetables is that they are very colourful. Cooked carrots have this very appetizing bright orange colour whereas broccoli exhibits a bright green colour in contrast. When I started making these vegetables, others too took note of the colourful vegetables that were on my plate.

Here is then an absolutely idiot-proof way of making sauté vegetables, and that too in a JIFFY.

Please feel free to use any seasonal European vegetable---- this list is only indicative.

Ingredients

Cauliflower-100 grams (3.5oz) (half cup)

Broccoli-100 grams (3.5oz) (half cup)

Carrot-100 grams (3.5oz) (half cup)

French beans-100 grams (3.5oz) (half cup)

Peas shelled or snow peas-100 grams (3.5oz) (half cup)

Butter-1 tablespoon

Water-2 tablespoon

Salt and Pepper to taste

Method

Wash the vegetables thoroughly.

Wherever needed, cut in bite size pieces.

Switch on your heat source and put a pan on it.

Add the butter to the pan and let it melt.

Add all the vegetables and stir well.

When the vegetables start changing colour, add a pinch of salt and keep stirring.

Reduce the heat to minimum (SIM on a gas stove), add the water and cover the pan.

You will see that the steam starts escaping after a while.

Keep checking till the water has dried.

Tip: You may also use a fork to poke the vegetables to ensure that they have been cooked properly.

Your sauté vegetables are ready. At this stage, you may like to add some pepper.

Preparation time: 5 minutes

Cooking time: 7 minutes

Total: 12 minutes

Sauté anything and everything

Congratulations!! Once you have learnt to sauté mixed vegetables, you can sauté anything and everything under the sun. You will need to follow the same steps as I indicated for the recipe on Sauté Vegetables and you just cannot go wrong. To recapitulate, here are the steps that you need to repeat every time you need to sauté anything:

Wash the veggies thoroughly and cut them into pieces wherever required.

Switch on your heat source and put a pan on it. Add a tablespoon of butter to the pan and let it melt.

Add your veggies and stir well.

When the vegetable starts changing colour, add a sprinkle of salt and keep stirring.

Reduce the heat to minimum (SIM on a gas stove), and add 2 tablespoon water.

Cover the pan with a lid.

You will notice the steam escaping after a while.

Keep checking till the water has dried.

Tip: Use a fork to poke the vegetable to ensure that it has been cooked properly. If the vegetable is tender that means your veggies are ready.

Prep time: 5 minutes

Cooking time: 7-10 minutes

Total time: 12-15 minutes

Learn to make a white sauce

If you are tired of eating sauté vegetables, then you might want to try something different. Learning to make a white sauce can add this much needed variety to your vegetarian dishes as you will soon see. This will also help you in making many other dishes with chicken, fish or pasta or whatever be your favourite ingredient.

Ingredients

Butter-1 tablespoon

Salt and Pepper to taste

Wheat flour–2 tablespoon

Milk-500 ml or 2 cups approximately (at room temperature)

Cheese Cheddar-50 grams or 2oz (3 tablespoon) (grated)

Method

Switch on your heat source and put a pan on it.

Add a tablespoon of butter to the pan and let it melt.

As the butter melts, add the flour.

Gently mix/sauté the flour with the butter making sure that the flour does NOT turn brown.

Switch off the heat source and let the mixture cool down.

When the mixture comes to room temperature, gently add the milk (also at room temperature) and mix well to ensure that no lumps are formed.

Return this to the fire.

Add the cheese and a bit of salt.

As soon as the mixture thickens, your white sauce is ready.

Graduate to Making Vegetables *au gratin*

This classic dish with a cheesy flavour is an all-time favourite. So if you liked the simple flavours of sauté vegetables, you can very easily graduate to Vegetables *au gratin*. The added protein and calcium from milk and cheese, that this recipe uses, increases this dish's overall nutrition quotient by many, many folds.

Note: Feel free to use any seasonal European vegetable---- this list is only indicative.

Ingredients

Cauliflower-100 grams (3.5oz) (half cup)

Broccoli-100 grams (3.5oz) (half cup)

Carrot-100 grams (3.5oz) (half cup)

French beans-100 grams (3.5oz) (half cup)

Peas shelled or snow peas-100 grams (3.5oz) (half cup)

Butter-2 tablespoon (1 tablespoon for sautéing vegetables and the other for making the white sauce)

Salt and Pepper to taste

Wheat flour–2 tablespoon

Milk-500 ml (2 cups; at room temperature)

Cheese Cheddar-50 grams or 2oz (grated) (3 tablespoon)

Method

First sauté the mixed vegetables, which means:

Wash the vegetables thoroughly.

Wherever needed, cut in bite size pieces.

Switch on your heat source and put a pan on it.

Add the butter to the pan and let it melt.

Add all the vegetables and stir well.

Tip: Please don't add salt to the vegetables because the white sauce will contain sufficient amount of salt.

Reduce the heat to minimum (SIM on a gas stove), add the water and cover the pan.

You will see the steam escaping after a while.

Keep checking till the water has dried.

You may also use a fork to poke the vegetables to ensure that it has been cooked properly. If the vegetables are tender that means it has been cooked well.

Your vegetables are ready. You can decorate your vegetables *au gratin* with finely sliced bell peppers which give it a nice flavour.

Next, Make the White Sauce, which means:

Switch on your heat source and put a pan on it.

Add a tablespoon of butter to the pan and let it melt.

As the butter melts, add the flour.

Gently mix/sauté the flour with the butter making sure that the flour does NOT turn brown.

Switch off the heat source and let the mixture cool down.

When the mixture comes to room temperature, gently add the milk (also at room temperature) and mix well to ensure that no lumps are formed.

Return this to the fire.

Add the cheese and a bit of salt.

As soon as the mixture thickens, your white sauce is ready.

Now add the vegetables to the white sauce and mix well.

Congratulations!! Your Vegetables *au gratin* is ready.

Preparation time; 10 minutes

Cooking time: 7 minutes

Total: 17 minutes

Lesson 7

HOW TO HANDLE CHICKEN

What should you buy whole or cut into pieces

Most places sell chicken as whole and also as cut in pieces. Weight wise, buying whole chicken could be cheaper than if you bought just chicken legs, or breasts or thigh pieces. You need the full chicken if you are making a dish like Roast Chicken and have access to an oven that can accommodate this. Otherwise, if you are just cooking for yourself and that too in a pan, then you may like to avoid the mess that you may make while cutting the chicken. The time saved will be another bonus.

How to Boil Chicken

For quite time, I was buying readymade chicken dishes such as Roast Chicken or Chicken Tikka Masala from supermarkets because I thought cooking chicken would be too complicated. Once I learnt to handle eggs and then vegetables, I had become confident enough to now experiment with chicken. I knew that boiling anything did not require any cooking skills and was the easiest thing to do. So, one day on Skype, I asked my mother, and here are those idiot-proof tips on how to boil chicken:

Ingredients

Chicken piece--1 (approx. 200-250 grams or 7-9oz (1 cup) with bones. Any piece, be it breast, leg, or thigh would do.)

Method

Since this recipe involves a chicken piece that weighs 200-250 grams (7-9oz) (1 cup) approximately, we are going to take 500 ml (2 cups approximately) water and pour the water in a pan.

Tip: If you wish to handle more chicken, then use more water in the ratio of one-and-a-half to two times to that of the chicken weight to ensure that your chicken cooks well but does not get burnt. For example, for a 250 gram (9oz) (1 cup) piece of chicken, use 500ml (2 cups approximately) water.

For a 500 gram (18oz) (2 cups) chicken, use 750-1000 ml (3-4 cups approximately) water and so on.

Submerge the chicken in the water inside the pan.

Place the pan on fire and let the water come to boil.

Reduce the heat and let the chicken simmer for about 10 minutes.

It is advised that you check that the chicken has been cooked properly. This can be done by using a fork to prick the chicken to see whether it has become quite tender.

Take the pan off from the heat source.

Once the water cools down, take the chicken out.

Tip: Don't throw away the water. This "chicken stock" can be used for making soups or gravies. If you don't want to do that immediately, you could just freeze this stock for future use.

That's all. Congratulations on learning how to successfully boil chicken. You have learnt the first important step of dealing with chicken and now the doors are open for you to experiment with this boiled chicken in an infinite variety of ways.

Why Should You Learn to Boil Chicken

You may be wondering that when boiled chicken in itself is so tasteless then why make all the effort in learning how to boil a chicken?

This is because boiling a chicken is the easiest thing you can do with chicken and though it does not taste good in itself, it gives you the confidence to follow a number of other recipes in a breeze. At least it did so for me. And in any case you have to start somewhere. Before you jump to making exotic dishes, mastering these basic skills will certainly make your task less daunting.

Now to the question as to what all you can you do with boiled chicken, well, you can use this chicken to make a delicious Chicken Sandwich or to make your favourite salad with the dressing of your choice. Combine it with white sauce and you can make Chicken in White Sauce without any difficulty. Once you are confident, you can easily advance to exotic recipes like Cold Chicken and really party with your friends. You can also use the chicken stock to make Chicken Soup or chicken gravy.

So don't scoff at the art of boiling chicken because this skill is going to lead to almost infinite possibilities of making dishes, whether from this book or from others.

Make a Delicious Chicken Sandwich

This is one of my favourite chicken dishes that I started making myself when I wanted to have something different during the weekends. To make this, you need to first learn how to boil and shred chicken, and then follow these instructions:

Ingredients

Boiled shredded chicken-100 grams (3.5oz) (half cup)

Mayonnaise-1 tablespoon

Dijon Mustard-1/2 teaspoon

A pinch of salt and powdered sugar

Bread-2 slices (of your choice)

Lettuce, tomatoes, cucumber or any other salad of your choice-Optional

Method

Boil the chicken in the same way that you have learnt. Since you cannot buy less than one piece of a chicken, therefore you can keep some boiled chicken for use later and use 100 grams (3.5oz) (half cup) of chicken to make the sandwich. We are assuming that a chicken piece weighs 200-250 grams (7-9oz) (1 cup) approximately, so we are going to take 500 ml (2 cups approximately) water and pour the water in a pan. To boil the chicken:

Submerge the chicken in the water inside the pan.

Place the pan on fire and let the water come to boil. Reduce the heat and let the chicken simmer for about 10 minutes.

It is advised that you check that the chicken has been cooked properly. This can be done by using a fork to prick the chicken to see whether it has become quite tender.

Take the pan off from the heat source. Once the water cools down, take the chicken out.

Now, shred the chicken piece. Mash the shredded chicken well along with a tablespoon of mayonnaise and Dijon Mustard.

Now, add a pinch of salt and one-fourth teaspoon of powdered sugar.

Spread this mixture on a slice of bread and add salads of your choice. Cover with another slice of bread and cut into two triangles.

Enjoy your chicken sandwich and be relieved that you don't need to buy one of those tasteless sandwiches from the supermarket ever.

Prep time: 5 minutes

Cooking time: 10 minutes (if boiled chicken is not available)

Total time: 15 minutes

Make Chicken In White Sauce

Once you have learnt to boil chicken and make a white sauce, you can easily make this recipe and surprise your friends.

Ingredients

Boiled shredded Chicken-300 grams (10oz) (1 + ½ cups)

Wheat flour--2 tablespoon

Milk-500 ml (2 cups approximately)

Cheese Cheddar-50 grams (2oz) (3 tablespoon)

Butter-1 teaspoon

Salt and Pepper-to taste

Method

Boil the chicken and shred it into bite size pieces. We are assuming that a chicken piece weighs 200-250 grams (7-9oz) (1 cup) approximately, so we are going to take 500 ml (2 cups approximately) water and pour the water in a pan. To boil the chicken:

Take 500 ml (2 cups approximately) water and pour the water in a pan.

Submerge the chicken in the water inside the pan.

Place the pan on fire and let the water come to boil.

Reduce the heat and let the chicken simmer for about 10 minutes.

It is advised that you check that the chicken has been cooked properly. This can be done by using a fork to prick the chicken to see whether it has become tender.

Now make the white sauce. In the previous chapter, we have already learnt how to make white sauce. To recapitulate:

Put the butter in a pan on the flame and after the butter melts, add the wheat flour.

Gently sauté the flour with the butter for a while. Always remember to ensure that the flour does NOT turn brown.

Switch off the heat source and let the flour cool down.

When it comes to room temperature, gently add the milk (also at room temperature) and mix well to ensure that no lumps are formed.

Return this to the fire, add the cheese and a bit of salt and pepper.

As soon as it thickens, your white sauce is ready.

Add the shredded chicken into this sauce. This dish goes really well with rice and canned pineapple slices.

Prep time: 5 minutes

Cooking time: 17 minutes (if boiled chicken is not available or otherwise it is 7 minutes)

Total time: 12-19 minutes

Can you believe it that you have actually made Chicken in White Sauce??? When this chapter began, we were not sure what you could do with raw or boiled chicken, and look where we have reached!

I was exactly like that. And now I can sense the excitement you would be feeling. Please do not worry if your dish doesn't come out perfect the first time. It will still, I am sure, be better than what is served in many Halls of Residences. So go ahead, and surprise/shock your friends with this dish.

Making Cold Chicken

This is a real party dish. You will not be able to resist the taste of chicken in white sauce, combined with the taste of fresh cream and fresh/canned fruits, and served chilled. You can really shock your friends and family members at this point, who a few months ago may be laughing at your rather non-existent cooking skills.

PLEASE NOTE THAT YOU SHOULD TRY THIS DISH ONLY WHEN YOU ARE CONFIDENT WITH THE OTHER PREVIOUSLY MENTIONED CHICKEN DISHES.

Are you ready to make this exotic dish? Then let's begin.

Ingredients

Chicken- 2 breast pieces

Wheat flour--2 tablespoon

Milk-500 ml (2 cups approximately)

Grated Cheese Cheddar-50 grams (2oz) (3 tablespoon)

Fresh Cream (Low fat)--100 ml (half a cup approximately)

Canned mixed fruit--1 small can

Butter-1 teaspoon

Salt to taste

Method

Boil the chicken in 500 ml (2 cups approximately) of water, the way you have already learnt, for 10 minutes. To reiterate, we are assuming that a chicken piece weighs 200-250 grams (7-9oz) (1 cup) approximately, so we are going to take 500 ml (2 cups approximately) water and pour the water in a pan. To boil the chicken:

Submerge the chicken in the water inside the pan.

Place the pan on fire and let the water come to boil.

Reduce the heat and let the chicken simmer for about 10 minutes.

It is advised that you check that the chicken has been cooked properly. This can be done by using a fork to prick the chicken to see whether it has become quite tender.

Take the pan off from the heat source.

Once the water cools down, take the chicken out and put it on a plate.

Save the stock (water that you used for boiling the chicken) for making soups or any other dish later.

Now make the white sauce that is, put the butter in a pan on the flame and after the butter melts, add the flour.

Gently mix the flour with the butter making sure that the flour does NOT turn brown.

Switch off the heat source and let the flour cool down.

When it comes to room temperature, gently add the milk (also at room temperature) and mix well to ensure that no lumps are formed.

Return this to the fire and add the cheese and a pinch of salt.

As soon as it thickens, your white sauce is ready.

In a bowl, whisk the fresh cream with a pinch of salt.

To this mixture, add the canned fruit.

In a big serving dish, place the chicken in the middle, each piece separately, 3and pour the white sauce over it. Put the canned fruit all along the sides.

Your delicious Cold Chicken is ready. You can eat it at room temperature if it is very cold or cool it in the fridge before serving if the weather is hot.

Prep time: 10 minutes

Cooking time: 17 minutes

Total time: 27 minutes

If you have been able to successfully replicate this dish, then you are a star cook or a chef by now.

Well done!! I have always stressed that you should not really bother if you feel that your dish was not "up to the mark". Just keep practicing and you will become perfect.

Don't give up. Always congratulate yourself that you attempted such an exotic dish and that too when, a few weeks ago, you did not even know how to boil a chicken. You really deserve applause.

Making a Breaded Chicken

If you have ever fancied making a KFC style chicken at home but with less calories, then this is the perfect recipe for lunch or dinner.

Ingredients

Boiled chicken piece-2 (any piece breast, leg, or thigh with or without bones)

Two slices of bread toasted and crushed into crumbs

Egg-1

Wheat Flour-1 tablespoon dissolved in half a small cup of water for coating the chicken

Salt-to taste

Utensils-Baking tray, oven, a bowl and a pan to boil the chicken

Method

Boil The Chicken:

Take 500 ml water and pour the water in a pan and add salt to taste.

Submerge the chicken in the water inside the pan.

Place the pan on fire and let the water come to boil.

Reduce the heat and let the chicken simmer for about 10 minutes.

It is advised that you check that the chicken has been cooked properly. This can be done by using a fork to prick the chicken to see whether it has been thoroughly cooked.

Now make the bread crumbs separately if you don't have it in ready stock. For making bread crumbs, you can take some left over bread which is already a little hard. Toast it well in the toaster. Take it out and let it cool down a bit. Then take a spatula to beat the toast till it all turns into crumbs.

Take the pan off from the heat source.

Now, take the chicken out once the water has cooled.

Break the egg by gently tapping the middle portion of the egg with a fork till a crack appears. Keep tapping till the crack becomes a small hole. Gently press the egg to break it into two halves. Pour the liquid in a bowl.

Mix the egg and wheat flour together and add a little salt.

In another plate, keep the crushed bread. Take the chicken piece one by one and coat them first in the egg and wheat flour mixture and then coat with the bread crumbs.

Put these on a baking tray and bake in a pre-heated oven at 150 degrees Celsius for 15 minutes.

Your non-deep fried, healthy Breaded Chicken is ready.

If you don't have access to an oven, you can simply deep fry the breaded chicken a´ la KFC.

Prep time: 20 minutes (if the chicken is not boiled and the bread crumbs have not been made)

Cooking time: 15 minutes

Total time: 20-30 minutes (depending upon what you have in ready stock)

How to Grill chicken

Ingredients

Chicken piece-1 (breast, leg or thigh)

Lemon juice-1 teaspoon

White Vinegar-1 teaspoon

Chopped garlic-2 pieces

Salt and pepper to taste

Butter-1 tablespoon

Method

Marinade the chicken piece by sprinkling one teaspoon lemon juice, one teaspoon vinegar, two pieces of chopped garlic and salt and pepper (to taste) on that piece.

Let the chicken marinade for half an hour. Don't worry if you have marinated the chicken for a longer time.

In a non-stick pan, add one tablespoon butter. When the butter melts, put the chicken piece in the pan and let it sizzle.

When the piece starts changing colour (that is when the raw look goes away, a whitish colour appears, before the chicken turns golden brown), gently turn it to the other side using a fork. In this way, you gently grill the chicken piece on both sides on low heat.

If the chicken still doesn't look cooked, add half cup water and cover the lid.

Remove the lid after two minutes and turn the piece. Do this till all the water evaporates and your chicken is nicely cooked and crisp on the outside.

PLEASE MAKE SURE THAT THE HEAT IS LOW AND THE CHICKEN DOESN'T BURN.

That's all. Your delicious Grill Chicken is ready.

Optional: In case, you have access to a Grill, you can put your chicken on a hot grill at the last stage of your cooking to get those wonderful grill lines.

Prep time: 30 minutes (because of marination)

Cooking time: 15 minutes

Total time: 45 minutes

Lesson 8

WHAT TO DO WITH FISH AND SEAFOOD

Once you are confident with handling chicken and cooking vegetables, you may want to try your hands on fish and seafood.

How to Grill a Fish

Ingredients

Boneless fish (any fish) fillet-2

Lemon juice-1 teaspoon

Chopped garlic-2 pieces

Salt and pepper to taste

Butter-1 tablespoon

Method

Sprinkle on the fish fillet the salt and pepper, lemon juice and chopped garlic.

Switch on your heat source and put a pan on it.

In the pan, add the butter and let it melt.

Add the fish fillet and on low heat let it grill on one side.

When fish starts acquiring a light golden colour, gently turn the piece and let the other side get the same colour.

You should be cooking on low heat so that the fish does not burn.

Turn it to a serving plate. Your grilled fish is ready.

Remember fish cooks very fast. You may still use a fork to prick the fish to ensure that the fish has been cooked properly.

You may buy some Tartar Sauce, Tomato Ketchup, Hollandaise Sauce or mayonnaise from the supermarket and enjoy your fish.

Prep time: 5 minutes

Cooking time: 7 minutes

Total time: 12 minutes

Making Fish Mayonnaise

This was one of my favourite ways to have fish. It is not difficult to replicate and is a bit similar to Cold Chicken (see Lesson 7: How to Handle Chicken).

This is how you go about:

Ingredients

Canned tuna-1

Mayonnaise-2 tablespoon

Fresh fruits and boiled vegetables of your choice e.g. apples, grapes, walnuts, cucumber, boiled peas, cauliflower, carrot, potatoes, etc.

Method

In a dish, take out the tuna from the tin and place it in the middle.

Cover the tuna with one tablespoon mayonnaise.

Chop all the fruits, salads and vegetables of your choice and mix it all with another tablespoon of mayonnaise.

Place all these around the tuna.

Your delicious fish mayonnaise with fruits is ready.

In case, you want to use fresh fish fillet then boil the same in one cup of water in a pan for 2 minutes with a little salt. This can then be used in the same manner as the tuna.

You have already learnt how to boil chicken in the previous chapter. Boiling fish is similar except that fish cooks faster and the water cannot be used for anything else. At least, I couldn't as it smelled too "fishy".

This is how you should boil fish:

Submerge the fish in one cup of water inside the pan.

Add a little salt.

Place the pan on fire and let the water come to boil.

Reduce the heat and let the fish simmer for about 2 minutes.

Take the pan off from the heat source.

Now, take the fish out once the water has cooled.

Prep time: 5 minutes

Cooking time: 5 minutes (if you are boiling fish; it will be faster if you are using canned tuna)

Total time: 7-10 minutes

Making Fish in white sauce

You should now be beginning to realize how making white sauce can come in so handy with any kind of dish. Simply boil your fish, pour on your own white sauce and voila, you have a lovely meal.

Ingredients

Boneless Fish Fillet Boiled-2 pieces

Butter-1 tablespoon

Salt and Pepper to taste

Wheat flour–2 tablespoon

Milk-500 ml (2 cups; at room temperature)

Cheese Cheddar-50 grams or 2oz (3 tablespoon) (grated)

Method

Boil the fish fillet and keep it aside.

This is how you should boil fish:

Submerge the fish in one cup of water inside the pan.

Add a little salt.

Place the pan on fire and let the water come to boil.

Reduce the heat and let the fish simmer for about 2 minutes.

Take the pan off from the heat source.

Take the fish out once the water has cooled.

Making the white sauce:

Switch on your heat source and put a pan on it. Add a tablespoon of butter to the pan and let it melt. As the butter melts, add the flour.

Gently mix/sauté the flour with the butter making sure that the flour does NOT turn brown.

Switch off the heat source and let the mixture cool down.

When the mixture comes to room temperature, gently add the milk (also at room temperature) and mix well to ensure that no lumps are formed.

Return this to the fire.

Add the cheese and a bit of salt.

As soon as the mixture thickens, switch off.

Your white sauce is ready.

Put the fish fillet on a plate and pour the white sauce over it. See that the fish is well covered.

Your fish in white sauce is ready to be served.

Prep time: 5 minutes

Cooking time: 10 minutes

Total time: 15 minutes

Making Fish Fry

If you want to be a little more adventurous, then you may like to try making Fish Fry.

Ingredients

Boneless fish fillet-2

Lemon juice-1 tablespoon

Crushed Garlic cloves-3

Crushed Ginger-1 inch piece

Egg-1

Wheat flour-1 tablespoon

Bread crumbs- made from 2 slices of toasted bread

Salt and pepper to taste

Oil for deep frying

Method

Marinate the fish fillet with lemon juice, crushed garlic, crushed ginger and salt and pepper. Leave the fillet for about 10 minutes.

Break the egg by gently tapping the middle portion of the egg with a fork till a crack appears. Keep tapping till the crack becomes a small hole.

Gently press the egg to break it into two halves. Pour the liquid in a bowl.

Mix the egg with the wheat flour.

In another plate, spread the bread crumbs.

To make bread crumbs, take some left over bread which is already a little hard. Toast it well in the toaster. Take it out and let it cool down a bit. Take a spatula and beat the toast till the toast is crushed and turns into crumbs.

Now, dip the fish fillet in the egg and wheat flour batter and then coat it with bread crumbs.

In a shallow pan, heat the oil till it is nice and hot.

Now, gently put the coated fish fillet into the same.

As one side of the fish browns, flip over (with the help of a spatula) and let the other side brown as well.

You should fry the fish one piece at a time.

Remove on to a plate on which you place a paper napkin. This will help absorb any excess oil.

Now turn into a serving dish and enjoy your fried fish with sauté potatoes or any vegetables of your choice, on the side.

You may use Tartar Sauce, Tomato Ketchup, Hollandaise Sauce or mayonnaise too with this fish.

Prep time: 5 minutes (if bread crumbs are ready. It is advised that you make bread crumbs and keep it as it can be used for a large number of dishes)

Cooking time: 5-7 minutes

Total time: 10-12 minutes

Making Prawns in tomato sauce

This was my most successful experimentation at Ifor Evans. When I had become confident enough with chicken, eggs and vegetables, I thought of playing around with prawns. I consulted my mom over Skype and discovered that this would be one of the easiest ways to handle prawns.

Believe me that it also tastes very good.

I felt really innovative after trying out this recipe. Now, you could also do the same.

Ingredients

De-shelled and de-veined Prawns (of your choice- tiger or shrimps)--500 grams (18oz) (2 cups)

Tomato sauce/ketchup-5 tablespoon

Butter-1 tablespoon

Salt and pepper to taste

Method

Switch on your heat source and put a pan on it.

In the pan, put one tablespoon butter.

Once the butter melts, add the prawns and gently sauté till prawns change colour, that is turn reddish.

Add the tomato sauce, salt and pepper and stir well.

Reduce heat and let the prawns simmer for about 2 minutes. Prawns leave a lot of juice. So there is no need to add any extra water.

Turn off the heat source and take out the prawns with the sauce on to a plate.

Your prawns are ready.

You can have on the side rice, bread, corn or sauté vegetables.

Prep time: 3 minutes

Cooking time: 7 minutes

Total time: 10 minutes

Graduate to making prawns with vegetables in tomato sauce

You have already learnt how to make prawns in tomato sauce. Now, you can simply add vegetables and easily graduate to this recipe.

Ingredients

De-shelled and de-veined Prawns (of your choice- tiger or shrimps)--500 grams (18oz) (2 cups)

Tomato sauce/ketchup-5 tablespoon

Soya sauce-1 teaspoon

Butter-2 tablespoon

Chopped Garlic-3 cloves

Sliced Onions-1

Sliced Bell Peppers-Red, yellow and green-50 grams (2oz) (3 tablespoon)

Carrots cut into small pieces-50 grams (2oz) (3 tablespoon)

Broccoli florets cut into small pieces-50 grams (2oz) (3 tablespoon)

Salt and pepper to taste

Method

Switch on your heat source and put a pan on it.

In the pan, put one tablespoon butter.

Once the butter melts, add the prawns and gently sauté till prawns change colour, that is turn reddish.

Take the prawns out into a plate.

In the same pan, add another tablespoon of butter and when it melts, add the garlic.

When the garlic splutters and gives off an aroma, add the other vegetables, except the peppers (red, yellow and green). This is because the peppers cook very fast and taste soggy if cooked for long.

Stir well. Reduce the heat and cover the pan allowing the vegetables to cook.

In case, the vegetables seem too dry, you can add 2 tablespoon water, so that the vegetables don't burn. This should all take about 3 minutes.

When the vegetables seem done to your taste, add the prawns, the peppers (red, yellow and green), the two sauces (tomato ketchup and soya sauce), salt and pepper and stir well together.

Let the mixture come to a boil. Reduce heat and cook for another minute. Turn off the heat source.

Your prawns with vegetables are ready.

Prep time: 5 minutes

Cooking time: 10 minutes

Total time: 15 minutes

Lesson 9

SOUPS AND SALADS

If you are fond of soups and salads then this lesson is for you. At the end of this lesson, you will be confident enough to experiment with as many kind of soup or salads as you like.

I have already mentioned how I survived on salads (which did not taste fresh) that I bought from the supermarket for the first few weeks of my UCL days. Had I known how to make my own salads, I would have certainly been not so miserable.

A lot of stores sell canned soup these days. Not only are they soulless but full of sodium (that increases your blood pressure) and many other harmful additives. Therefore, the purpose of this lesson is to make you independent where soups and salads are concerned, and to help you avoid many of the troubles that I had to so unnecessarily go through.

How to Make Chicken Stock

In the previous chapters, we have already spoken a lot about boiling chicken. The left over water after boiling a chicken is called chicken stock. You can easily make a soup out of this left over water when you have boiled chicken for any other dish.

For making chicken stock for one person, we assume that you will be boiling a chicken piece approximately the size of 200-250 grams (7-9oz) (1 cup), so we are going to take 500 ml (2 cups approximately) water and pour the water in a pan.

Method

Submerge the chicken in the water inside the pan. Place the pan on fire and let the water come to boil.

Reduce the heat and let the chicken simmer for about 10 minutes.

It is advised that you check that the chicken has been cooked properly. This can be done by using a fork to prick the chicken to see whether it has become tender.

Take the pan off from the heat source. Take the chicken out once the water has cooled. Use this water, called "Chicken Stock" to make any kind of chicken soup—a basic chicken soup, chicken sweet corn soup or French onion soup. You don't believe me? So, just read on.

Making a Basic Chicken Soup

Ingredients

Chicken stock—2 cups

Boiled shredded chicken-50 grams (2oz) (3 tablespoon)

Grated Cheese-25 grams (1oz) (1 + 1/2 tablespoon)

Milk-1/2 cup

Corn Flour-1 heap tablespoon full

Salt and Pepper to taste

Sugar-1/2 teaspoon

Method

Pour the chicken stock in a pan.

Add the cheese, sugar and salt.

Switch on your heat source and put the pan on it.

Bring this mixture to a boil.

Meanwhile, dissolve the corn flour in half a cup of milk separately.

Add this to the mixture in the pan to give it a nice creamy taste.

Boil for 2 more minutes and add the shredded chicken.

A trick is to taste the soup to see whether the salt is alright or whether you need to add a little more.

Your chicken soup is ready.

You may freeze the extra soup to consume it at a later date.

Prep time: 5 minutes

Cooking time: 10 minutes

Total time: 15 minutes

Graduate to Making Chicken Sweet Corn Soup

Once you have learnt how to make a basic chicken soup, you can make Chicken Sweet Corn Soup without any difficulty. This is because the two recipes are very similar to each other and the only difference is that you put an egg and corn in making Chicken Sweet Corn Soup.

Ingredients

Chicken stock—2 cups

Boiled shredded chicken-50 grams (2oz) (3 tablespoon)

Egg-1

Corn Kernels-50 grams (2oz) (3 tablespoon)

Corn Flour-1 heap tablespoon full

Salt and Pepper to taste

Sugar-1/2 teaspoon

Method

Pour the chicken stock in a pan.

Add the corn kernel, sugar and salt.

Switch on your heat source and put the pan on it.

Bring this mixture to a boil.

Meanwhile, dissolve the corn flour in half a cup of milk separately.

Add this to the mixture in the pan to give it a nice creamy taste. Boil for 2 more minutes and add the shredded chicken.

Break the egg by gently tapping the middle portion of the egg with a fork till a crack appears. Keep tapping till the crack becomes a small hole. Gently press the egg to break it into two halves.

Pour the liquid in a bowl and beat the egg lightly with a fork.

As the chicken stock is boiling, slowly pour the beaten egg and stir well. This will help thicken the soup and also spread the egg evenly.

A trick is to taste the soup to see whether the salt is alright or whether you need to add a little more.

Your Chicken Sweet Corn Soup is ready.

You may like to add a little vinegar and soya sauce if you like to make it a little tangy and "Chinesey". Otherwise you can have it as it is, the British way.

Either way, this is quite a filling dish.

Prep time: 5 minutes

Cooking time: 7 minutes

Total time: 12 minutes

Now Pass Out with Honours with French Onion Soup

This is quite the ultimate soup that you could make with chicken stock. Here's the recipe:

Ingredients

Chicken stock-2 cups

Sliced Onions-2 large

Cheese slices-2

Salt to taste

Sugar-1/2 teaspoon

Butter-1 tablespoon

Method

If you have chicken stock, use it. Otherwise you can make it by the method indicated in "How To Make Chicken Stock" at the beginning of this lesson.

In a deep pan, add the butter and put it on the fire.

As the butter warms up, add the sliced onions and stir well till the onions start browning.

Reduce the heat and sprinkle the sugar on the onion. This helps the onions become really nice and brown and getting a nice caramelized taste without burning.

Add the chicken stock and the salt and let this mixture boil.

Pour into 2 microwavable soup bowls.

In each bowl, place a slice of cheese and microwave for 2 minutes.

In case you don't have access to a microwave, then place the cheese first in the bowl and pour boiling soup over it. This is done so that the slice of cheese melts yet retains its shape.

Our home made variation of French Onion soup is ready.

This dish tastes really nice with a crisp garlic bread.

Prep time: 7 minutes

Cooking time: 12 minutes

Total time: 19 minutes

Making Soups for the Vegetarians

Once you have learnt to sauté vegetables (*see Lesson 6: How To Cook Vegetables*), then this category of soups will be a breeze for you.

Making Mixed vegetable soup

Ingredients

French beans-50 grams (2oz) (3 tablespoon)

Carrots-50 grams (2oz) (3 tablespoon)

Potatoes-1 (peeled)

Broccoli/Cauliflower-50 grams (2oz) (3 tablespoon)

Wheat flour-1 heaped tablespoon

Milk-1/2 cup

Butter-1 tablespoon

Salt and pepper to taste

Water-2-3 cups (depending upon how thick you like the soup. Less water will make the soup thicker and more will make the soup lighter)

Method

Chop finely all the vegetables.

In a deep pan, add the butter and put it on the fire.

As the butter melts, add all the vegetables and stir well.

When the vegetables start changing their colour, add the wheat flour and again stir well for 2 minutes.

Now, add the milk, water, the salt and pepper. Let the mixture boil.

Reduce the heat and cook till the vegetables are done.

That's all. Your healthy vegetable soup is ready in a jiffy.

Prep time: 5-10 minutes (depends if you need to cut vegetables)

Cooking time: 10 minutes

Total time: 15-20 minutes

Making Soups for the Slightly Adventurous

If you are in the mood to try out something new, then you may want to try making a pumpkin soup or tomato soup.

I MUST WARN THAT BOTH THESE SOUPS REQUIRE A BLENDER. SO THEY MAY BE A LITTLE COMPLICATED FOR A NEWBIE.

Making Pumpkin soup

Ingredients

Ripe yellow pumpkin-250 grams or 9oz (1 cup) (all chopped up)

Onion-1 (chopped up)

Garlic-2 cloves

Cinnamon powder-1 teaspoon

Milk-1/2 cup

Water-2 cups

Butter- 1 teaspoon

Salt to taste

Method

In a deep pan, put the butter and add the chopped onions and garlic.

Put it on fire and sauté till the onion is translucent.

Add the chopped up pumpkin and stir well.

Add 2 cups of water and bring the mixture to boil.

Reduce the heat to minimum (SIM if on gas) and cook till the pumpkins become soft.

Switch off the heat and let the mixture cool down.

Put this mixture in a blender and blend well.

Strain this all back into the pan.

Add the cinnamon powder, milk and salt and bring to a boil.

Switch off the heat and serve.

It is suggested that you taste the soup before serving so that you may adjust the salt according to your taste.

Your simple yet exotic pumpkin soup is ready.

You may want to freeze the left over portion of the soup for future consumption.

Prep time: 10 minutes

Cooking time: 15 minutes

Total time: 25 minutes

Making Tomato Soup

Ingredients

Ripe Tomatoes-500 grams or 18oz (2 cups) (chopped up)

Onion-1 (chopped up)

Garlic-2 cloves (chopped up)

Ginger-1 inch piece (chopped up)

Milk-1/2 cup

Corn Flour-1 heap tablespoon

Salt, sugar and pepper- to taste

Water—2 cups

Method

Put all the chopped up ingredients (EXCEPT MILK, SALT, SUGAR AND CORN FLOUR) in a deep pan along with 2 cups of water.

Put the pan on fire.

After the mixture starts boiling, reduce the heat and cook till the tomatoes are well cooked (approximately 7 minutes).

Switch off the heat source and let the mixture cool down.

Take out the mixture and blend it well in a blender.

Strain this mixture back into the pan and bring it to a boil.

Add the corn flour, dissolved in half a cup of milk.

Add also the salt, pepper and sugar.

Let the mixture boil for 2 minutes.

Turn off the heat source.

Your lovely homemade tomato soup is ready.

It is suggested that you taste the soup before serving so that you adjust the salt and sugar according to your taste.

Prep time: 8 minutes

Cooking time: 10 minutes

Total time: 18 minutes

Making Basic Salad

Ingredients

Anything you want to put in the salad like lettuce, Brussels sprouts, cucumber, corn, cherry tomatoes, apples etc.

Vinegar-1 tablespoon

Fresh lemon juice-1 tablespoon

Honey-1 tablespoon

Salt and pepper to taste

Method

In a bowl, mix together all the fruits and vegetables.

In another small bowl, mix together the vinegar, lemon juice, honey, salt and pepper.

Pour this mixture into the salad bowl and mix well with all the ingredients.

Your healthy tasty salad is ready.

Prep time: 5 minutes

Cooking time: No cooking time

Total time: 5 minutes

Making Hawaiian Chicken Salad

Ingredients

Chicken Ham/Sausages/Salami of your choice-2 slices

Cheese cube-2

Canned pineapple-2 slices

Apple-1

Cucumber-1/2

Roasted Peanuts-1/2 small cup

Mayonnaise-1 tablespoon

Sprinkling of Salt to taste

Method

Chop all ingredients into bite size pieces (EXCEPT PEANUTS) on a cutting board.

Put all the ingredients in a bowl and mix together with the mayonnaise and salt.

Mix well.

Sprinkle the peanuts on top.

Your Hawaiian salad is ready.

If you are a vegetarian, then just remove the ham (keep all other ingredients intact).

If you don't take eggs too, then try out an eggless/vegetarian mayonnaise.

Prep time: 5 minutes

Cooking time: No cooking time

Total time: 5 minutes

Concluding notes

I hope by now, you would have got a general drift of making different soups and salads. You would have also got an idea to creatively mix different ingredients to make a salad of your own choice. Please do not hesitate to try out any combinations that you think your taste buds will just love and let your creative juices flow freely.

Lesson 10

MAKING A FULL MEAL IN 30 MINUTES WITH PROPER SEQUENCING AND PARALLEL PROCESSING

Don't be alarmed with the use of such big words as "sequencing" and "parallel processing". This is no rocket science because unconsciously we all continuously "sequence" our actions and do "parallel processing".

When you wear your socks before slipping into your shoes, haven't you just "sequenced" your actions in a very logical manner? And who doesn't walk while listening to music---but then you just indulged into some "parallel processing", howsoever ill-advised it may be, especially when you are walking with traffic around you.

Cooking is no different, except that you probably don't know how with proper sequencing and parallel processing you can reduce your drudgery by many, many folds.

The Concept of Full Meals and Parallel Processing

One major obstacle to cooking is that most of us do not have enough time. We have to rush to our office or college or Gym, prepare for tutorials or hang out with friends. In the process, cooking becomes a chore and a casualty.

Even when we are able to cook something, we rarely have the satisfaction of having a full balanced meal. Sequencing and parallel processing allows us to plan our meals in such a manner that while one dish is getting ready, we can make the others. This little planning in advance can reduce both the cooking and preparation time considerably and enable you to prepare a full 3-4 course meal literally in a JIFFY.

The examples given below are only suggestive. Once you get the hang of the "philosophy" I'm talking about, you can come up with any number of your own permutations and combinations, I'm sure.

A WORD OF CAUTION THOUGH. YOU MUST FAMILIARISE YOURSELF WITH THE DISHES MENTIONED IN THIS LESSON BEFORE

ATTEMPTING TO SEQUENCE AND PARALLEL PROCESS THEM. IN THIS WAY YOU WILL NOT ONLY BE EFFICIENT BUT AVOID LOTS OF CONFUSION.

Making a Full Breakfast in less than 15 minutes

We provide here the sequencing and parallel processing for making a breakfast of scrambled eggs, sauté peas, grilled tomatoes, and your favourite beverage in less than 15 minutes.

To refresh your memory, here are the individual recipes first:

Sauté peas

Ingredients

Peas Shelled-200 grams (7oz) (1 cup)

Butter-1 teaspoon

Water-2 tablespoon

Salt to taste

Method

Wash the peas thoroughly.

Light the fire and put the pan on it.

Add the butter and let it melt.

Add the peas and stir it well.

When the peas start changing colour, add the salt.

Reduce the heat, add the water and cover the pan.

You will see that the steam starts escaping after a while.

Keep checking till the water has dried.

Please ensure that your peas don't burn or become mushy. Your sauté peas are ready.

Grilled tomatoes

Ingredients

Tomato-1 cut in half

Butter-1/2 teaspoon

Salt and Pepper to taste

Method

Wash the tomato thoroughly before cutting.

Cut the tomato in half.

Light the fire and put the pan on it.

Add the butter and let it melt.

Place the tomato cut side down and let it sizzle for a minute.

Turn it around and give it another minute.

Put it in a plate and sprinkle salt and pepper.

Scrambled egg

Ingredients

Egg-1

Milk-1 tablespoon

Butter-1 teaspoon

Grated Cheese-1 tablespoon

Salt and Pepper-Just a sprinkle

Method

In a non-stick pan, gently tap the upper portion of an egg to make a small hole for you to pour the liquid in the pan comfortably. Please be careful and ensure that no portion of the egg shell goes into the pan. There is no need to separate the egg yolk from the egg white.

Now put the rest of the ingredients in and mix it all well.

Put the pan on your cook stove and switch on the heat source.

Immediately reduce the heat to medium.

Stir the mixture continuously ensuring that the mixture neither STICKS TO THE PAN NOR BURNS.

As soon as the mixture cooks (that is when there is no liquid left), switch off the heat source and while stirring continuously, pour the mixture onto a serving plate.

Remember if the mixture becomes too dry or lumpy, it will no longer taste creamy and if the mixture remains too wet, it will give a raw taste.

Tip: A common pitfall is to add more milk than suggested or to forget to put the milk altogether. In both cases, the scrambled egg will NOT taste as good as we want it to be.

Tip: Another pitfall is to add a lot of salt. This recipe requires just a pinch of salt and pepper because butter and cheese already contain some salt.

Let's now come to the sequencing and parallel processing needed for your breakfast:

For the scrambled egg, take a non-stick pan, and mix all the ingredients together in it. Don't put this on fire as yet.

Next, make the peas in a separate pan.

After removing the peas on to the plate, make the roasted tomato in the same pan.

Now put the toast in your toaster and switch that on (if you want toasts with your eggs).

Switch on your coffee/tea machine (if you like a hot beverage) or pour yourself a glass of your favourite juice.

Now make the scrambled egg.

Your toast would have popped out by now.

Your full (and healthy) breakfast of scrambled egg with toast, sauté peas, roasted tomato with your favourite beverage is ready.

This whole effort should not take you more than 15 minutes.

You can always add some sinful sausages and bacon to have a proper British breakfast, which may take you another 5 minutes.

Or in the same time, you could add boiled frankfurters or ready- to- eat ham or salami if you really want to have a lavish five-star breakfast.

Have a happy daybreak.

Making a Full Lunch or Dinner in less than 30 minutes

Similarly for lunch or for dinner, you may use the art of proper sequencing and parallel processing to make Chicken soup, breaded baked chicken, sautéed vegetables and garlic toast in less than 30 minutes. Don't believe it. Let me prove it to you then.

To refresh your memory, let us recapitulate the individual recipes first:

Basic Chicken Soup

Ingredients

Chicken stock—2 cups

Boiled shredded chicken-50 grams (2oz) (3 tablespoon)

Grated Cheese-25 grams (1oz) (1 + 1/2 tablespoon)

Milk-1/2 cup

Corn Flour-1 heap tablespoon full

Salt and Pepper to taste

Sugar-1/2 teaspoon

Method

Make the chicken stock by boiling chicken using the following method:

Take 500 ml water and pour the water in a pan and add salt to taste.

Submerge the chicken in the water inside the pan.

Place the pan on fire and let the water come to boil.

Reduce the heat and let the chicken simmer for about 10 minutes.

It is advised that you check that the chicken has been cooked properly. This can be done by using a fork to prick the chicken to see whether it has been thoroughly cooked.

Take the pan off from the heat source.

Now, take the chicken out and keep it on a separate plate once the water has cooled.

Shred some portion of the chicken into bite size pieces (50 grams or 2oz or 3 tablespoon) and keep the rest for your breaded baked chicken.

Keep the chicken stock in the same pan.

Add the cheese, sugar and salt.

Switch on your heat source and put the pan on it.

Bring this mixture to a boil.

Meanwhile, dissolve the corn flour in half a cup of milk separately.

Add this to the mixture in the pan to give it a nice creamy taste.

Boil for 2 more minutes and add the shredded chicken.

A trick is to taste the soup to see whether the salt is alright or whether you need to add a little more.

Your chicken soup is ready.

Breaded Baked Chicken

Ingredients

Boiled chicken piece-2 (any piece breast, leg, or thigh with or without bones)

Two slices of bread toasted and crushed into crumbs

Egg-1

Wheat Flour-1 tablespoon dissolved in half a small cup of water for coating the chicken

Salt-Just a pinch

Utensils-Baking tray, oven, a bowl and a pan to boil the chicken

Method

First, make the bread crumbs if you don't have it in ready stock. For making bread crumbs, you can take some left over bread which is already a little hard. Toast it well in the toaster. Take it out and let it cool down a bit. Then take a spatula to beat the toast till it all turns into crumbs.

Break the egg by gently tapping the middle portion of the egg with a fork till a crack appears. Keep tapping till the crack becomes a small hole. Gently press the egg to break it into two halves. Pour the liquid in a bowl.

Mix the egg and wheat flour together and add a little salt.

In another plate, keep the crushed bread. Take the chicken piece one by one and coat them first in the egg and wheat flour mixture and then coat with the bread crumbs.

Put these on a baking tray and bake in a pre-heated oven at 150 degrees Celsius for 15 minutes. Your non-deep fried, healthy Breaded Chicken is ready.

If you don't have access to an oven, you can simply deep fry the breaded chicken a´ la KFC.

Sauté Vegetables

Please feel free to use any seasonal European vegetable---- this list is only indicative.

Ingredients

Cauliflower-100 grams (3.5oz) (half cup)

Broccoli-100 grams (3.5oz) (half cup)

Carrot-100 grams (3.5oz) (half cup)

French beans-100 grams (3.5oz) (half cup)

Peas shelled or snow peas-100 grams (3.5oz) (half cup)

Butter-1 tablespoon

Water-2 tablespoon

Salt and Pepper to taste

Method

Wash the vegetables thoroughly.

Wherever needed, cut in bite size pieces.

Switch on your heat source and put a pan on it.

Add the butter to the pan and let it melt.

Add all the vegetables and stir well.

When the vegetables start changing colour, add a pinch of salt and keep stirring.

Reduce the heat to minimum (SIM on a gas stove), add the water and cover the pan.

You will see that the steam starts escaping after a while.

Keep checking till the water has dried.

Tip: You may also use a fork to poke the vegetables to ensure that they have been cooked properly.

Your sauté vegetables are ready. At this stage, you may like to add some pepper.

Garlic Toast

Ingredients

Bread-2 slices preferably cut thick (you can use any bread, or even bun of your choice)

Garlic-5 cloves crushed

Salted Butter-20 grams (1oz) (1 tablespoon)

Any fresh green herb of choice

Method

In a pan, warm up the butter and add the crushed garlic.

Let it cook for a minute and then switch off.

Meanwhile, toast the bread (or bun) well.

Spread the garlic mixture on the toast.

You can sprinkle any fresh herbs on this toast.

Your delicious garlic bread is ready.

Let's now come to the sequencing and parallel processing needed for your lunch or dinner

First of all, gather all your ingredients and vessels.

Then begin with the soup.

While the soup is cooking, sauté the vegetables in a separate pan and toast the bread for the breaded baked chicken.

Once this is done, toast the bread/bun lightly for the garlic toast.

While the chicken soup is cooling down, transfer the vegetables to a casserole.

Finish the soup and put it in a casserole if you want the soup to remain piping hot.

Make the breaded chicken and put it in the oven.

Make the butter + garlic spread. Put the spread on the toast for the garlic toast.

Take out the chicken from the oven.

Your lunch/dinner is ready in a JIFFY, in less than 30 minutes.

You can make lots of dishes with your boiled chicken, many of which do not require an oven, and substitute that dish for the breaded chicken. This will add more variety to your lunch/dinner menu without much effort. Some of these recipes have already been discussed in *Lesson 7 on "How to Handle Chicken"*.

Parting Tips.......

How Not To Turn Cooking Into a Chore

I see this as more of an attitudinal problem. If you consider cooking to be a dreadful experience, you will always like to keep yourself away from the kitchen. In that sense, as I have said earlier, it is very much like working out.

People give up on their work outs basically because they don't ENJOY it. They see exercising as some kind of a torture. On the other hand, people who fall in love with working out never become tired of their fitness regime.

It is the same with cooking.

I personally found cooking to be magic. For me, it was a very refreshing break—both from studies and work. I really enjoyed seeing the vegetables and seafood change colour inside the pan.

The fact that I could make whatever I liked to have and whenever I wanted to, gave me a real sense of power, pleasure, and freedom. With the money saved from cooking at home, I could occasionally indulge myself by buying exotic fruits, veggies or seafood that would otherwise cost a bomb in any restaurant.

Coming back to my "working out" analogy, you can reduce the perceived drudgery of cooking (or working out) by first, teaming up with a friend or a partner.

Secondly, by having some music or TV playing in the background.

And finally, by following the sequencing and parallel processing tips that I share in this Book that I guarantee will help you create a full three course meal from scratch in less than 30 minutes.

What If Things Go Horribly Wrong In the Kitchen

Have you ever feared that your friends or family members might call your cooking "a ball of poo", or that you will either undercook or overcook or simply burn whatever you be cooking, or that your pot/pressure cooker/kettle will probably explode due to overheating?

I must tell you that you are not the only one. I had similar fears when I started cooking. But I am sure that you will almost always be able to find a tiny voice inside you that encourages you to experiment and explore. Listen to that tiny voice and I bet that nothing will go wrong.

People (and that includes professional cookbook writers and celebrity chefs) needlessly make cooking extremely complicated. Let me tell you that cooking the kind of food that your mom makes (and that you really love) cannot be all that hard.

So what if you struggled breaking eggs the first time and dropped two tiny pieces of eggshell into your omelette? I would say making an effort is the greatest thing.

When I started cooking my own meals, I was proud of the fact that I could make my own meals. I had full control over my meals and I could ensure that my nutrition did not suffer.

When you browse through the various chapters of this book, you will realize how much I struggled initially. The first time I made my scrambled egg, it came out lumpy because my stirring was not effective. But it had to get better with time and effort.

You should also not give up. See cooking as a learning experience and an opportunity to explore a new skill and I bet nothing can ever go horribly wrong for you.

Still, to be extra safe, please do invest in a portable fire extinguisher and a first aid kit and keep them handy.

See that your heat source is not left on unnecessarily or accidentally.

Please ensure that you don't put an empty non-stick pan on the fire and then look for the ingredients that have to go into it because that will spoil your non-stick coating in no time.

Before you use any device, be it a blender, oven, or microwave, please go through its instruction manual and keep those manuals in a special drawer to keep them readily accessible.

All perfectly common sense advice that I am sure you don't need me to unnecessarily expound upon.

Concluding tips

I hope you have enjoyed reading this book as much as I enjoyed writing it.

If you are beginning to think that this book was very basic, then I must congratulate you on having learnt the basics of cooking. You must give yourself a pat on the back for learning and internalising all the basics of cooking so much so that now you may want to venture out and challenge yourself.

At this point, I may as well give you another small tip. If you are looking for more challenges, then why not try making Thai Green curry, Indian recipes or desserts, which are all available free-of-cost from my website *www.cookinginajiffy.com*.

You are now qualified to experiment with any kind of cooking that you wish to, be it from this book or from some other cookbook or website. I encourage you to do that.

This is the only way you can hone your cooking skills and who knows some day you may start cooking like a professional chef. And yes feel free to adapt the recipes as per your style and convenience.

I wish you all the best with your cooking endeavour.

Other Books by the Author

Home Style Indian Cooking In A Jiffy

With an amazing compilation of over 100 delectable Indian dishes, many of which you can't get in any Indian restaurant for love or for money, this is unlike any other Indian Cook book. What this book focuses on is what Indians eat every day in their homes. It then in a step-by-step manner makes this mysterious, never disclosed, "Home Style" Indian cooking accessible to anyone with a rudimentary knowledge of cooking and a stomach for adventure.

Prasenjeet Kumar, the corporate lawyer turned gourmand, in this second book of his series "How to Cook everything in a Jiffy" explores the contours of what sets Indian "Home Style" food so apart from restaurant food . In his uniquely semi-autobiographical style, he starts with his quest for

Indian food in London, wonders why his European friends don't have such a "strange" debate between "Home Style" and "Restaurant" food, and learns that the whole style of restaurant cooking in India is diametrically opposed to what is practised in Indian homes with respect to the same dish.

You may like this book if:

You are an Indian pining for a taste of your home food anywhere in the world, including India.

You are an Indian, reasonably adept in your own regional cuisine, for example, South Indian cuisine, but want to learn about the "Home Style" culinary traditions of the Eastern and Northern India as well.

You are NOT an Indian but you love Indian cuisine and have wondered if someone could guide you through the maze of spices that Indians use, and help you tame down the oil and chilli levels of many of their dishes.

Recommends Amazon.com Top 100 Reviewer Penmouse "There's plenty to like concerning the Home Style Indian Cooking In a Jiffy cookbook by author Prasenjeet Kumar. Kumar has formatted the book so each recipe links back to the interactive table of contents making navigation easy. He's also included color photos illustrating his recipe throughout his cookbook.

Best of all Kumar offers information how to set up a basic kitchen, a brief introduction to Indian spices and goes onto offer various chapters covering Indian food.

His recipes offer both the standard cooking method or the option to use a pressure cooker (when appropriate) to prepare the recipe. He gives clear directions how to complete the task using either cooking method..."

Connect with the Author

This book has been written, I believe, in such a way that even an absolute newbie should not have any problems following it. However, if you do encounter some problem or find any portion confusing, then feel free to write to me anytime at *ciaj@cookinginajiffy.com*.

If you liked this book and want to hear from us again regarding news of upcoming books or if you wish to receive weekly recipes and cooking tips from us, then you may want to subscribe to our blog. You can do that by simply going to our website *www.cookinginajiffy.com/squeeze-page/*.

I would love to connect with you on Social Media. Join me on Facebook (*www.facebook.com/cookinginajiffy*) or follow me on Twitter (*www.twitter.com/CookinginaJiffy*) or Goodreads (*www.goodreads.com/prasenjeet*).

About the Author

Prasenjeet Kumar is a Law graduate from the University College London (2005-2008), London University and a Philosophy Honours graduate from St. Stephen's College (2002-2005), Delhi University. In addition, he holds a Legal Practice Course (LPC) Diploma from College of Law, Bloomsbury, London.

Prasenjeet loves gourmet food, music, films, golf and traveling. He has already covered sixteen countries including Canada, China, Denmark, Dubai, Germany, Hong Kong, Indonesia, Macau, Malaysia, Sharjah, Sweden, Switzerland, Thailand, UK, Uzbekistan, and the USA.

Prasenjeet is the self-taught designer, writer, editor and proud owner of the website *www.cookinginajiffy.com* which he has dedicated to his mother.

Please review my book

If you liked my book then I shall be grateful if you could leave a review on the site from where you purchased this book and show your support.

Index

Basic Chicken Soup, *143*

Basic Omelette, *71*

Basic Salad, *155*

Boil an Egg, *53*

Boil Chicken, *106*

Bread Crumbs, *46*

Breaded Chicken, *119*

Cheese Garlic Toast, *48*

Cheese Omelette, *73*

Chicken In White Sauce, *112*

Chicken Sandwich, *109*

Chicken Stock, *142*

Chicken Sweet Corn Soup, *145*

Coffee, *44*

Cold Chicken, *115*

Concept of Full Meals and Parallel Processing, *160*

Egg Fry, *66*

Egg Poach, *69*

Egg Sandwich, *55*

Fish Fry, *132*

Fish in white sauce, *129*

Fish Mayonnaise, *127*

French Onion Soup, *147*

French Toast Salted, *76*

Garlic Toast, *47*

Grill a Fish, *125*

Grill chicken, *122*

Grilled Egg Sandwich, *57*

Grilled tomatoes, *87*

Hawaiian Chicken Salad, *156*

Mixed vegetable soup, *149*

Peel a Perfect Boiled Egg, *53*

Prawns in tomato sauce, *135*

prawns with vegetables in tomato sauce, *137*

Pumpkin soup, *151*

Sauté anything and everything, *97*

Sauté baby potatoes, *89*

Sauté Mixed Vegetables, *94*

Sauté peas, *85*

Scrambled Egg, *62*

Soups for the Slightly Adventurous, *151*

Soups for the Vegetarians, *149*

Spinach with butter, *91*

Sweet French Toast, *79*

Tea, *41*

Toast, *45*

Tomato Soup, *153*

Vegetables *au gratin*, *101*

white sauce, *99*

Printed in Great Britain
by Amazon